Auer and Blumberg have lent their insight, passion, and compassion to this workbook. In so doing they have also provided a guidebook—and a preamble of advocacy for children and their families.

—Morton Ann Gernsbacher, Ph.D., Vilas Research Professor and Sir Frederic C. Bartlett Professor of Psychology at the University of Wisconsin-Madison

It has been said that a family of five is akin to five people lying side-by-side on a waterbed: whenever one person moves, everyone feels the ripple. A child with sensory processing disorder can have a devastating impact upon the day-to-day functioning of a family. There are several books available that provide data and information on the nature of this puzzling disorder, but Auer and Blumberg have written a valuable book that finally provides parents with specific strategies and practical solutions to the daily challenges faced by these special children and their families. While other books define the problem, Auer and Blumberg offer techniques to minimize the effect of the disorder on the child's daily life. I strongly recommend this book to any adult who is parenting a child with a sensory processing problem—and to the professionals who are assisting moms and dads on this challenging journey.

—Richard D. Lavoie, M.A., M.Ed., author of *It's So Much Work to Be Your Friend* and executive producer of *How Difficult Can This Be? The F.A.T. City Workshop*

Finally a book that treats SPD in the full context that it deserves: not as a co-condition or as another obstacle but as a full fledged challenge to the complete inclusion of individuals with unique learning styles. The collaborative integration of the senses accounts for your picking up this book, examining it and deciding on whether to make it part of your library. Auer and Bloomberg walk you through how that process is both derailed and rekindled.

—Rick Rader, MD, editor-in-chief of *Exceptional Parent* magazine and director of the Morton J. Kent Habilitation Center

Read this with a highlighter in hand, because you will want to refer many times to the wise and wonderful ideas in this splendid how-to book. The authors are not only sensitive and resourceful parents of kids with SPD, but also articulate, honest, and sensible writers.

—Carol S. Kranowitz, MA, author of
The Out-of-Sync Child

In raising children with or without special needs, nothing is more important than the family unit. This book will enable you to enhance your child's sensory development. Additionally, it will help you ensure that your child and all family members not only survive, but, indeed, thrive! When your whole family thrives, you can best ensure your child's optimum development over the short and long range of life.

—Ann Turnbull, Ed.D., cofoounder and
codirector of the Beach Center on Disability
at the University of Kansas

Parenting a Child *with* Sensory Processing Disorder

A Family Guide to Understanding & Supporting Your Sensory-Sensitive Child

CHRISTOPHER R. AUER, MA,
WITH SUSAN L. BLUMBERG, PH.D.

New Harbinger Publications, Inc.

Publisher's Note

This publication is designed to provide accurate and authoritative information in regard to the subject matter covered. It is sold with the understanding that the publisher is not engaged in rendering psychological, financial, legal, or other professional services. If expert assistance or counseling is needed, the services of a competent professional should be sought.

"The Role of Therapy in Treatment of Children with Sensory Processing Disorder" in chapter 1 was printed with permission from Bridget Bax.

"Sanctified Near Sightedness" and "Go to the Mosquito, Thou Dejected" by Frederick S. Miller in chapter 2 are reprinted from *Verses from Korea* (1937) with permission from the Christian Literature Society of Korea.

"Evan's Story" in chapter 2 was printed with permission from Susan Perry Simpson.

"A Father's Point of View" in chapter 4 is printed with permission from J. Neil Tift.

"Jordy's Story" in chapter 4 is printed with permission from Doug Gertner.

"The Sibling Experience: Unique Concerns, Unique Opportunities" in chapter 5 is printed with permission from Don Meyer.

"A Sibling's Point of View" in chapter 5 is printed with permission from Donna Batkis.

"A Cultural Perspective for Families of Children with Special Needs" in chapter 6 is printed with permission from Jane Delgado.

The story "Holland Schmolland" in chapter 7 is reprinted from www.parentmentors .org with permission from Laura Crawford.

"A Child 'At Promise'" in chapter 7 is printed with permission from Kathy Marshall.

"Ideas to Support Your Child with SPD Outside of Traditional Therapy" in chapter 8 is printed with permission from Michelle Auer.

Copyright © 2006 by Christopher Auer
New Harbinger Publications, Inc.
5674 Shattuck Avenue
Oakland, CA 94609
www.newharbinger.com

Cover design by Amy Shoup; Cover image: Sigrid Olsen/PhotAlto/Getty Images (models only, used for illustrative purposes); Acquired by Tesilya Hanauer; Edited by Amy Johnson;

Library of Congress Cataloging-in-Publication Data

Auer, Christopher R.
  Parenting a child with sensory processing disorder : a family guide to understanding and supporting your sensory-sensitive child / Christopher R. Auer, with Susan L. Blumberg.
      p. cm.
  ISBN-13: 978-1-57224-463-4
  ISBN-10: 1-57224-463-1
  1. Children with disabilities—Family relationships. 2. Parenting. 3. Sensory integration dysfunction in children. I. Blumberg, Susan L., 1959- II. Title.
HQ773.6.A84 2006
649'.152—dc22   2006028311

08   07   06
10   9   8   7   6   5   4   3   2   1
First printing

Contents

Acknowledgments

Susan and I wish to thank all of the contributors to this book—parents, children, and experts. Specifically, we thank Jane Delgado, president and CEO of the National Alliance for Hispanic Health; Don Meyer, director of the Sibling Support Project of the Arc of the United States; J. Neil Tift, director of professional advancement, National Practitioners Network for Fathers and Families; and Kathy Marshall, executive director of the National Resilience Resource Center.

This book started out as nothing more than an idea to write something to help families coping with the challenges of parenting a child with sensory processing disorder (SPD). Lucy Miller both provided important encouragement and explained the entire process of getting a book published. She is one of the most giving people I (Chris) have ever met.

I am grateful, too, for literary agent Jody Rein. She spent many hours answering my questions and guiding me through the process of getting a book published—not to mention negotiating the final contract.

This book could not have been written without the help of my coauthor Susan Blumberg. Susan reminded me—and kept reminding me—to make this book personal and write as a parent. On several occasions, she deleted entire pages with suggestions of a different direction. She was always right. I appreciate her honesty, integrity, and skill; I can't imagine a better partner.

At New Harbinger Publications, I am especially grateful to Tesilya Hanauer. Tesilya not only has great skill as an editor, she also has remarkably expedient follow-through. Thanks also to Heather Mitchener and Carole Honeychurch for their editing skill, and to publicist Earlita Chenault.

Deep gratitude must also go to Pamela Harris, my supervisor, both for her support of this project and for her understanding and patience on days when I was out of it due to a late night of writing. Thanks also to Maria Guajardo Lucero for inspiration and the teaching of cultural proficiency.

I cannot possibly thank my wife Michelle, an occupational therapist, enough. She is the most important person in my life. Michelle took far more than her share of responsibility in the home so that I could write. She also managed to at least appear to listen to me talk endlessly about this book. Michelle makes me whole.

I am also indebted to my children Lauren, Brendan, and Evan. Without them, I wouldn't have nearly as many good stories to tell. All three of them are smart, fun, and compassionate.

My father provided a tough example of a parent for me to follow; he never gave up on any of us. My mother instilled compassion and the love of learning. Lastly, my brother Tom gave me encouragement and constructive feedback; my brother Roger gave me an incredible story of hope and perseverance.

—Christopher Auer

I (Susan) thank Chris for the wonderful year of thoughts and ideas and friendship we shared while writing this book. My daughter Aviva has made the life of my family much more interesting—this book has been a wonderful way to celebrate all we have learned since her birth. I'd also like to thank my son Nathan and my husband Lewis, for their patience while I was writing and their love and understanding while I was rewriting. Also, my parents; they are an unending source of love and support and I love them deeply.

—Susan L. Blumberg

Foreword

Four key things to know about sensory processing disorder (SPD):

1. Something really *is* wrong when a child has SPD—symptoms aren't just figments of imagination.

2. SPD *is* real, even though many people do not "believe" in it.

3. Early identification of SPD is critical to prevent the occurrence of secondary problems, such as poor social participation, poor self-regulation, and poor self-esteem/ self-confidence.

4. Something *can* be done if the disorder is accurately diagnosed.

Since training with Dr. A. Jean Ayres, originator of the field of sensory integration, I've spent more than thirty years working with children who have SPD and their families. As a teenager, I experienced a traumatic sensory disorder (not SPD but one related to an ocular disease); the doctor told my parents that nothing was wrong, it was all just in my head. As a result of having to cope with my slowly degenerating eyesight while not being believed, I developed secondary problems with self-esteem and relationships. These experiences led me to focus my career on the research and early identification of SPD.

Research shows that SPD affects 5 percent of children in the United States—and yet it isn't recognized formally in either the *Diagnostic and Statistical Manual of Mental Disorders* (DSM-IV) or the *International Classification of Diseases* (ICD-10). Though it seems impossible today, there was a time that neither of these standard classification indices recognized autism or ADHD either. In fact, it wasn't until the publication of the DSM-III-R in 1987 that the terms autistic disorder and ADHD were officially sanctioned.

This doesn't, of course, mean that autism and ADHD didn't exist before they were officially authorized as "real disorders" by the DSM. They simply weren't recognized or understood. This is where SPD stands today—and why books like this one are so important to the advancement of our care for our children with SPD.

In this book, Chris Auer and Susan Blumberg offer an important, fresh perspective on SPD. The focus of this innovative book is on nurturing relationships to positively impact both the child with SPD and each member of the child's family. Releasing internal stress through talking openly and knowledgeably about the child's disorder is presented as the key to accord. Whole family involvement is highlighted with chapters on strategies for nurturing relationships between partners, positive coping strategies for siblings, and the importance of the father's role. Into each topic, the authors subtly weave explorations of the power and strength that one's culture brings.

Sensory processing disorder is a family affair; children suffer and parents despair. We realize that others don't understand us. Our family relationships become the most meaningful fabric of our lives. In this book, Chris and Susan help us to understand this in new ways.

In addition to reviewing the internal resources needed by both children with SPD and the parents of these children, the authors also address the importance of external resources. A core theme of this book is learning strategies to communicate with professionals successfully, and learning to navigate systems so that families can receive the best culturally relevant care available.

Advocacy is key to a child's success, and knowledge is power. Parents who push without knowing their rights are likely to be turned away and to create enemies at schools and doctor's offices—but parents who are informed about their rights under the law, have a well-developed rationale for their requests, and can communicate positively yet assertively are more likely to receive the support their child needs. Parents who are informed can make a huge difference in their child's access to services and supports.

This book, the first of its kind for children with SPD, will give power and knowledge to the parents of children with SPD. It is a must-have reference for all of those parents.

Intervention for SPD isn't just about improving sensory processing, it's about improving quality of life: improving play with other children, improving self-confidence, and helping children with SPD so that families *all together* can do the activities they desire.

What can *you* do? Well, that's the topic of this compassionate book. I highly recommend reading it—and, if you can, becoming involved in larger SPD advocacy efforts as well.

—Lucy Jane Miller, Ph.D., OTR
Director, Sensory Therapies and Research (STAR)
Center Executive Director, The KID Foundation
Author of *Sensational Kids: Hope and Help for Children with Sensory Processing Disorder* (2006)

Introduction

CHRIS'S STORY

After I entered the lodge for our staff retreat, my supervisor took one look at me and doubled over with laughter. No, I hadn't worn my pajamas to work (my personal recurring nightmare). The cause of laughter was a thick dark circle around my eye, the result of an encounter with my then four-year-old son Brendan. It's safe to say that I lost that encounter. I wore my battle scar for about two weeks, to work, to the grocery store, to Sunday dinner with my father.

The encounter led to an emotional and painful awakening: we needed assistance. As a family, we were being pushed down a path none of us had volunteered for. But surely, it seemed, if any family was capable of meeting the needs of our child it was ours. My wife works for one of the local school districts as an occupational therapist and I work with families and children with special needs. In addition, I can also relate as a sibling to a brother with autistic behaviors; I'm very well aware of the challenges a family encounters when one member has a disability. How then could we be struggling so much? Why was it so difficult?

At the time we didn't know what was wrong with Brendan. When we mentioned the difficulties we were facing to our child's pediatricians (we changed several times out of frustration), the usual response was "Preschool-age children are normally very active," or "He'll grow out of it." We felt like grabbing a bullhorn and shouting as loud as we could, "Houston, we have a problem!"

Many doctors we spoke to agreed that Brendan displayed some symptoms of attention-deficit/hyperactivity disorder (ADHD), but found additional behaviors not typically associated with this disorder. Because he didn't fit the typical pattern, doctors were reluctant to make a diagnosis—or even give us a referral for additional assessment. Furthermore, they explained that a diagnosis of ADHD isn't usually made until a child is at least five years old.

Finally, we managed to see a child psychiatrist, and—with Brendan literally climbing the walls of the office, hitting his sister, and throwing the psychiatrist's books on the floor—this doctor diagnosed him with ADHD. My wife and I felt a sense of relief and validation. It wasn't us. We weren't incapable parents.

However, over time we recognized that there was really much more to Brendan's symptoms than just ADHD. He was constantly craving sensory input—his senses were totally out of whack. Brendan constantly gritted his teeth and would grab the arms or legs of anyone within a hundred yards (especially his siblings), squeeze, and press his lips against the other person's skin, blowing and sometimes even biting.

He was also over-responsive to smells and bright light. We felt like we'd given birth to a vampire: Brendan screamed inconsolably whenever the sun was on his face. Brendan also struggled with transitions, especially changing seasons. As summer turned to fall, Brendan would insist (forcefully) on wearing shorts and a T-shirt outside—even when it was thirty degrees. He didn't seem to notice or care about the cold. Eventually, with a lot of coaxing, he was able to transition to a turtleneck, snow boots, and sweatpants—until early summer, when again we faced a tough transition.

One beautiful warm spring day, as I carried Brendan in his turtleneck, snow boots, and sweatpants into church, he covered both ears with his hands and complained that church was too loud. I looked at all of the other children sitting with their families in the pews. While the other children seemed to be enjoying the music, Brendan was in pain. At this moment, it was clear to me that something was different with Brendan, beyond ADHD—so different that Brendan couldn't participate in daily activities. I realized then that we had to set out again to find help for Brendan and our family.

SUSAN'S STORY

When Aviva turned two-and-a-half, her occupational therapist Nina proudly reported that she no longer had to wash quite as many of the toys after Aviva's visits, that Aviva was now finding ways to explore the toys other than just put them in her mouth. I breathed a sigh of relief—I'd always felt bad watching Nina follow Aviva around with a spray bottle and a roll of paper towels.

Afterwards, I realized how odd this moment was. After all, at two-and-a-half most children are playing with markers, clay, and sand. Aviva couldn't have any of those things—they just went straight into her mouth. When there was nothing else around, she sucked her fingers—not her thumb, *all* of her fingers and all at once. She needed constant stimulation. We got her a small massager with a giant button she could push, so she could rub it on her arms and legs. She would also do repeated laps around the dining room table—once she even made it up to twenty-three!

The only way we could get Aviva to fall asleep was to let her lie full-length on our chests, holding her until she was soundly asleep. She slept in our bed from the time she was a year old, because we got tired of the two-hour screaming fits in the middle of the night—and my husband Lewis grew *really* tired of watching Barney videos every night. If we could touch and cuddle her as soon as she started to stir, we all could fall back asleep more quickly. She slept with us for nearly two years, until her third birthday, when she proudly graduated to a toddler bed.

Aviva's constant need for stimulation and touch was exhausting. She had to be rubbed and held to calm her down after any difficult moment. And even with regular physical and occupational therapy, starting when she was eleven months-old, Aviva was extremely clumsy. She would push her doll carriage in one direction while looking in another—and then fall off the curb in yet a third direction. Her right hand didn't seem to know what her left foot was doing!

When Aviva was eighteen-months-old, her occupational thera-pist gave us a copy of a chapter on sensory integration disorder from *The Out-of-Sync Child* by Carol Stock Kranowitz. It was amazing—it described Aviva perfectly. We were both relieved and stunned at the same time. We now had a label that made sense, but a prognosis that was very guarded. We couldn't know then how much this would affect her life—and our lives—forever. We had only just begun our journey to find the help that Aviva would need.

THE CHALLENGES OF PARENTING A CHILD WITH SPD

Both of us found it surprisingly difficult to apply our professional knowledge to our families. We each had to struggle not only to identify our child's behaviors, but also to find the right experts, programs, and services. Part of the problem is that sensory issues take many forms and are often poorly understood by the medical and educational systems in our country. A recent study suggests as many as one in twenty children may have sensory processing disorder (SPD) (Ahn et al. 2004). These children experience touch, taste, smell, sound, and sight very differ-ently than typical children. Further research indicates that many chil-dren with other conditions— including autism, fragile X syndrome, and ADHD—may also have sensory issues (Miller et al. 2001; Miller et al. 1999; Wang, Wang, and Ren 2003).

However, even though research demonstrates that many children have these kinds of sensory issues, SPD still isn't included in the stan-dard references from which insurance companies, physicians, and psy-chologists derive diagnoses. As a result, it's difficult for families to obtain appropriate treatment and care for their child with SPD; often, even if families do obtain the right kind of care, insurance companies simply won't pay for it.

Parents of children with SPD encounter similar obstacles to get-ting help that parents of children with ADHD encountered twenty years ago. Imagine describing the symptoms of your child's SPD to a pediatrician, only to be told that medication is the only option. Imag-ine being told by school staff that your child just needs to try harder—when you know that she needs specialized help. Imagine how even more difficult getting help for a child with SPD is for a family living in poverty or speaking a language other than English.

Support systems—including health care, schools, mental health providers, and community services—still have much to accomplish in terms of providing appropriate, culturally competent assistance while recognizing the unique strengths of each individual family.

WHY WE WROTE THIS BOOK

In our own journeys to help our own children, we've read many books, looked at many Web sites, and talked to many therapists. Although the books currently available about SPD offer an excellent understanding of SPD, they don't tell you how to identify and build upon your existing family strengths.

We wanted to take a different approach, to write a book about the things that our families needed beyond diagnoses and therapists. We wanted a book that would positively impact all members of the family. This book is designed to help you find the resources you need, understand the current state of the research about SPD, and—most simply—learn the questions you should be asking to help your family.

The health of your family and your child's outcome are linked. If your family is healthy, your child will have a better chance to be healthy. Similarly, if your child is doing well, it's easier to have a strong family. The purpose of this book is to enable you to identify your family's strengths, establish a strong foundation, and use this as a base to better parent your child with SPD.

WHO THIS BOOK IS FOR

Anyone closely involved in raising or supporting a child with SPD can benefit from reading this book. Both parents who suspect their child may have SPD but don't have a formal diagnosis and parents who've already had a diagnosis confirmed can benefit from this book. Our focus is to provide practical ways to support the child with SPD in the context of the family. We believe this to be more important than focusing on providing therapeutic activities for the child alone. While the emphasis of this book will be on ways to support your child in the home, we'll also provide information to help you obtain appropriate professional support. Professional support complements the care that you provide in your home, so your child receives help on all levels.

HOW TO USE THIS BOOK

We hope this book will become a well-used companion—dog-eared, highlighted, and penciled. Don't feel obliged to read it cover-to-cover. Instead, pick it up when time allows and read those chapters of interest to you.

This book is intended to be interactive; we've woven activities throughout the chapters to help you master the ideas presented. We've also presented many family stories to help you understand how the larger ideas might relate to your life. At the end of each chapter, a brief conclusion summarizes chapter information for later reference.

Many of the chapters also include the perspective of a respected authority on issues related to the needs of a child with SPD. You'll find information from these authorities in boxed text. These individuals include: Jane Delgado, president and CEO of the National Alliance for Hispanic Health; Don Meyer, director of the Sibling Support Project of the Arc of the United States; Neil Tift, director of professional advancement, National Practitioners Network for Fathers and Families; and Kathy Marshall, executive director of the National Resilience Resource Center, University of Minnesota. We thank them for all of their expert advice.

We've divided the writing of this book between us as follows: Susan has written the chapters on relationships (chapter 3) and resilience (chapter 7) and has added her stories and perspectives to many of the issues this book explores. The remainder of the book has been written by Chris. Thus, the "I" in most of the first-person stories in this book will refer to Chris; when the voice switches, it will be clearly stated or appear in boxed text.

Chapter 1 will provide you with the basic language you need to talk to others about your child, whether they're family members or professionals. While the information in this chapter is sometimes somewhat technical (though as much as possible, it's explained in easy-to-understand terms), stories add the personal touch to make the information more relevant to you and your child.

Chapters 2 through 7 focus on the topics of marriage, siblings, father involvement, culture, communication, and resilience, all viewed through the lens of SPD. These chapters will give you the skills and knowledge needed to build the strong, united family that will carry you through the many challenges you will face together. This is the heart of the book. Truly, in order to be a parent-leader, you need to know your family's assets—and be able to tap into all of your sources of strength when things get difficult. Everyone in your family is impacted by SPD; everyone in your family should be involved in making things better.

You (mothers and fathers) will develop a vision for your family's future. You'll learn to talk openly about SPD, so that all family members will understand how this disorder impacts the family and be able to respond appropriately. You'll learn to recognize and address the needs and emotional responses your other children may have as siblings of a child with SPD. You'll learn how mothers and fathers respond differently to the pressures of having a child with SPD. You'll learn, too, both how to improve your communication with your spouse and how fathers can become more involved.

Chapters 8 and 9 will teach you the strategies and skills you need to use the information presented in the previous chapters to build a strong, healthy family. We'll talk about stress and healthy ways of coping. We'll talk about the financial impact of parenting a child with SPD and finding alternatives to expensive therapy. We'll talk about loneliness and isolation. And, finally, we'll talk about the power of sharing your story. Sharing your story can be not only a source of inspiration for other families, but also a source of healing for your family.

WHAT YOU NEED TO GET STARTED

To get started you'll need three things: First, you'll need a journal. You want to have something that's appealing to write in, something that sets the mood for reflection. Choose something that suits your personality—or write a blog if that suits you better. If you detest writing (and it's okay if you do), consider recording your thoughts and reflections instead. If you're an artistic person, you might want to draw pictures in response to the exercises and activities. Record your thoughts and feelings in a way that's meaningful to *you*.

Second, get yourself a good tool for recording information (pen, pencil, paintbrush, tape recorder, etc.). For example, you might prefer to journal with a high quality fountain pen. The point is to get yourself in the right frame of mind in whatever way suits your personality.

Third—and probably most difficult—give yourself time and space. You'll need time and space to read the book, reflect upon the questions and exercises in this book, and dialogue with your spouse/partner/whomever helps you care for your child. Time to yourself might be at night after everyone else is in bed; a space of your own might be your car, a corner of the dining room, or just your favorite chair. Finding your time and space is a wonderful first step to helping yourself and your family.

FINAL THOUGHTS

Sometimes we all need to reflect on the journey. My family's journey has been bumpier than I (Chris) ever imagined it could be—but that means it has not just downs, it also has some really wonderful ups. For example, a couple of weeks ago, when asked what he was proud of about himself, Brendan explained with great pleasure that he is "smart and hyper." This statement represents an enormous achievement: Brendan now has a strong sense of self. He knows about his strengths and uniqueness as a human being.

So remember: even when your journey is difficult, it can also be successful. This book will give you and your family the skills and strengths necessary to help create these successes.

Chapter 1

An Overview of Sensory Processing Disorder

Raising a child presents challenges to any family, under any circum-stances. Imagine the challenges of parenting a child who:

- Screams when you show affection by softly patting her on the back

- Gags on most foods, including such typical crowd-pleasers as hot dogs and macaroni and cheese

- Hits, bites, pinches, and grabs—not out of ill will; he just can't help it

- Cannot learn to swim because whenever her face gets wet she cries inconsolably

Sensory processing disorder (SPD)—sometimes known as sensory integration disorder—affects approximately 5 percent of all children.

Although this may not at first sound like a lot, it means there are, on average, one or two children with SPD in every class—as far as disorders go, that's a pretty large number. There's also clear evidence that many children with autism, attention-deficit/hyperactivity disorder (ADHD), fragile X syndrome, and many other disorders also have sensory processing issues.

Children with SPD can have difficulty learning and may be shunned by their peers. If you're a parent of one of these children, you may not know what name to give to the behaviors you're seeing in your child, but your instincts are probably telling you, quite loudly, that something isn't right.

What's in a name? A lot. My brother Roger displays some autistic behaviors. He's never, however, had a formal diagnosis. Some professionals have thought he suffers from schizophrenia; others have been convinced he has autism; still others have shrugged their shoulders and confessed they just don't know. Without even this much of a name, I wouldn't be able to explain my brother's behaviors to anyone. A name provides understanding.

When my parental instincts began telling me something was wrong with my son Brendan, I couldn't put a name to it. I now know that my son has both ADHD and SPD. To me, that's reassuring in a strange sort of way. Names validate your instincts and your concerns. Names confirm that the behaviors you're dealing with are real—and not just limited to you. This chapter is meant to provide you with a name.

HOW WE PROCESS SENSORY INFORMATION

The theory of sensory integration was pioneered by Jean Ayres (1920–1988). Ayres defined *sensory integration* as the neurological process that organizes sensory information from the body to allow it to function effectively within its environment. In order to function in our environment, we need our brains to filter and interpret vast amounts of information. All aspects of sensory information are associated, interpreted, and unified in the brain (Kinnealey and Miller 1993); the brain receives a tremendous number of sensory details every moment of every day. When sensory information is interpreted correctly, we know where our body is in relation to other objects, when we can relax, and when we need to be alert; we can even focus on a specific task, filtering out all unnecessary information, whether it's the scratching of our neighbor's pencil or the chirping of the birds outside.

From the time that we begin to grow in our mother's womb our body receives and processes sensory information from our environment in order to function and learn. However, many children don't process sensory information correctly. Over the years this disorder—or dysfunction—has been termed dysfunction in sensory integration (DSI), sensory integration dysfunction (SID), and, more recently, sensory processing disorder (SPD). (For a more detailed history of the term, log on to the KID Foundation Web site [see the resources section at the back of the book].)

I will use the term SPD throughout this book; SPD is not only the term currently used in research, it's also an umbrella term that includes all three distinct patterns associated with the disorder (discussed later in the chapter).

When Senses Are Out of Whack

A child with SPD may over- or under-respond to sensory information, have difficulty coordinating muscle movements, or be unable to appropriately interpret sensory information coming into the body.

Once, on a family outing, we were making our way through a mall when there was a deafening scream. I looked at my children. My youngest son, Evan, was screaming and crying; Brendan stood beside him looking very nervous—the kind of nervousness that comes from guilt. Looking closer, I saw deep bite marks in Evan's arm. Before I could respond, Brendan explained—with complete sincerity—that he couldn't help it; he'd needed something to bite, and apparently Evan's arm was the closest (and tastiest) thing he could find.

In this example, Brendan was doing his best to protect himself. All of the sensory information of the mall (noise, colors, movement of people, etc.) overwhelmed Brendan to the point that his body began to have a fight-or-flight reflex. As a method of coping, Brendan did what his body was telling him to do: bite. (Adults do this too: when my wife gets nervous, she bites her nails, a habit that drives me crazy; when I get nervous, I play with my ear—which drives *her* crazy.)

Sometime during the primary grades, children are taught the five senses. To refresh your memory (mine needed refreshing, too), the five senses are: taste, touch, hearing, smell, and sight. We use these senses both individually and in tandem to interpret and learn about our environment.

During my preparation to become a teacher, I was taught the importance of using multisensory instruction. Effective teachers teach concepts through as many different senses as possible. For example, to teach spelling, a teacher might have children say the word, see the word, and then write the word in shaving cream with their fingers. Thus these children would experience this word through three different modalities or senses: hearing, sight, and touch. When children (and adults) have the opportunity to learn a concept through a variety of senses, they're far more likely to understand it and remember it.

From the moment a child is born, everything about the world is learned through the senses. But what if your child's sensory system is out of whack? Imagine a child who appears normal but is very sensitive to touch. Using the spelling lesson example again, for this child even just lightly touching the shaving cream may be painful, provoking a fight-or-flight protective response—which might be flinching, crying, or hitting the nearest person. Not surprisingly, then, modifications to the classroom environment may be necessary for this child to learn appropriately.

YOUR CHILD'S SENSORY SYSTEM

There are seven senses critical to the healthy functioning of your child's overall sensory system, the five we're taught about in school plus two more (overviews of all seven senses are provided below). When a sense doesn't interpret information as it should, a problem can result. As you read about each sense, think about how your child functions in this area. Does your child touch everything? Is your child scared of certain noises? These clues can help your family develop strategies to support your child at home, in school, and in the community.

Taste and Touch

Taste and touch are the most basic of the senses; together, they're known as the *tactile system*. Infants learn about their environment by putting everything—including toes, fingers, crayons, dirt, dog food, and anything else that they can get their hands on—into their mouths. With a normal tactile system, infants are able to learn through trial and error about different textures, what tastes yummy, and what doesn't.

As with the other sensory systems, the tactile system manages both protective factors and discriminative factors. For the tactile system, *protective factors*—such as temperature, light, and touch—alert us to potential dangers. For example, when we start to eat a piece of moldy bread, our sense of taste kicks in and stops us, protecting us from food that could cause us harm. A child with a poorly functioning tactile system may interpret most tactile experiences as potentially dangerous, and therefore avoid these experiences.

The tactile system's *discriminative factors* tell us about the things we touch. We learn by discriminating among different objects and identifying their respective qualities—whether that be size or texture. For example, toddlers begin to learn about shapes (circles, triangles, etc.) by playing with them and matching them with corresponding holes. Preschool children learn about volume by filling containers with sand or water. Discriminative factors also help us learn what is safe—e.g., sandpaper is rough and raspy and may hurt us if we rub it too hard, while sponges are soft and squishy (some children with SPD find sponges and sandpaper equally unpleasant).

Hearing

Sound can affect children with SPD in two different ways: First, for a minority of children, noise levels themselves can be a major problem. For example, Brendan experiences the sound of a congregation singing like an assault.

Second, auditory processing can be a problem. *Auditory processing* refers to how we receive and interpret sounds. A child with poor auditory processing skills may have a very difficult time using and understanding language. Rhyming is a crucial preliteracy skill that teaches the child to discriminate sounds. By rhyming "sound" with "pound," we can teach a child to identify not only sounds that are the same ("ound" in this case) but also sounds that are different ("s" versus "p"). However, a child with poor auditory processing skills may not be able to make these discriminations. A speech-language pathologist could work with such a child to enhance the child's ability to use and understand language.

Children with SPD may also have difficulty staying calm enough to listen to a set of directions given verbally—especially in a noisy classroom—and may not be able to successfully organize the auditory information they receive to follow the directions. Not surprisingly, this can lead to long-term educational problems.

Smell

Smell seems to be the least researched sense in regard to SPD. However, anecdotally, many parents report that their children are just as sensitive to smells as they are to touches and tastes. Many parents describe having to use unscented detergent on their children's clothes or be careful about the spices they use in cooking; some children with SPD can't even stand to stay in the room with someone smelling of a strong scent or even just certain shampoos. If your child is unable to verbalize his reason for needing to leave a room—or just seems unhappy—you may want to consider smell as a possible cause.

Certain odors, such as lavender, vanilla, and rose, have also been found to calm children, while the scents of peppermint and lemon can help children wake up. Try some bath oil or body lotion in small amounts to see if your child likes any of these. However, be careful: everyone has different scent preferences and certain smells may not work for your child.

Sight

Vision comes from information taken in through the eyes then processed by the brain. *Visual processing* refers to how the brain does its interpreting work, not the mechanics of the eyes (e.g., a visual processing problem isn't something that can be solved by a new pair of glasses). *Visual-spatial relations* refers to the positions of objects in space and the ability to figure out where things are in relation to other objects; visual-spatial skills include such things as copying problems from a blackboard onto paper, completing puzzles, buttoning buttons, tying shoelaces, and writing.

A child with poor visual-spatial processing may have trouble differentiating between shapes. Since letters are essentially just shapes, this can make reading and spelling a real challenge. For example, the typed versions of p, q, d, and b cause millions of children anguish. The shape of these letters is the same; the only difference is in orientation. A child with poor visual discrimination abilities would definitely have a difficult time learning to recognize these letters; and most likely others as well. The same can also be true of numbers; lining up long addition or multiplication problems can be particularly challenging for children with poor visual-spatial processing.

The Vestibular System

The *vestibular system*, associated with the inner ear, is responsible for the orientation and movement of the body in relation to gravity; it allows us to determine whether we're moving or our surroundings are. The vestibular system also tells us when we've had enough movement, whether we're driving down winding roads or sailing the seven seas. If we don't listen, we get sick—usually enough to get us to listen to our body and stop moving.

The vestibular system also controls a host of other functions, including motor planning and coordination. When this system is affected by SPD, children may have difficulty playing sports, finding their way around new places, and walking up or down stairs. For example, Susan's daughter Aviva experiences walking down stairs as a feeling of falling.

A vestibular system that's out of whack can also impact the back-and-forth movements of the eyes. As a result, a child may have difficulty aiming her eyes when reading from one word to the next. The ability to track or follow an object in motion can also be affected.

Motor Planning

Motor planning refers to our conscious control of our muscle movements. When we first learn a skill, we have to consciously plan our movements. For example, the first time we sit in front of a keyboard, our fingers don't have any idea what to do. We usually have to look at the keyboard, figure out where the letters are, consciously move our finger to the correct letter, and then inform the finger that it's okay to push that key. Over time, these movements become semiautomatic and we no longer have to make any conscious effort. The same is true when children first learn to write. Similarly, learning to do things like play the piano can also be difficult for kids with SPD, because it requires them to both read music and watch where their fingers are at the same time.

Coordination

There are two different types of coordination: bilateral coordination and crossing-midline coordination. *Bilateral coordination* is the ability to control both sides of our body together. It's interesting to observe a child with poor bilateral coordination. A child with poor bilateral coordination really functions as if there are two unrelated parts to her body. For example, Aviva, like many children with SPD, has great difficulty riding a bike. She has no sense of which side of her body is working, and thus must watch her feet to see which one should pedal next—which can understandably make it a little difficult to see where to steer!

Crossing-midline coordination is the ability to perform actions across the center of our body. Brendan is unable to cross his midline. When Brendan's occupational therapist instructs him to draw a large plus sign on the paper, he first draws a vertical line with his right hand, then switches the pencil to his left and draws a horizontal line from the left side of the page to the vertical line, then switches the pencil back to his right hand and draws a line from the vertical line to the right side of the page.

Proprioceptive System

The *proprioceptive system* is a network of receptors in muscles and joints that enables us to identify our body position in relation to other people and objects. Information received by these receptors tells us where our body parts are and what they are doing. As you can imagine, this is helpful information to have! Children who have poor proprioceptive systems appear clumsy and may slouch in their seats. In fact, they often slide right off their chairs and end up on the floor.

Children who have poor proprioceptive systems may also require different input to the receptors in their muscles and joints in order to feel comfortable. For example, Brendan has always had a difficult time sleeping comfortably. At the age of two, we, like many parents, transitioned him from his crib into a big-boy bed. He's never slept a complete night in this bed. One night, tired of awakening in the middle of the night with a foot, head, or arm in our faces, my wife and I had had enough. We presented Brendan with a choice. He could sleep in our walk-in closet, in the playpen we still had set up for our youngest son, or in his own bed in his room. Of course, we naively assumed that Brendan would choose his room. Brendan chose the playpen, and has slept there peacefully ever since, with five thick blankets on top of him.

I now understand that the playpen is an ideal place to sleep for Brendan, given his poor proprioceptive functioning. For one, the playpen provides a clear definition of space, which is comforting. For another, because Brendan is big enough that he has to sleep curled up in a fetal position, the playpen provides needed input (compression) to the receptors in his muscles and joints. On top of that, his five blankets provide weight, and thus add even further input to his sense of body awareness and security.

SENSORY PROCESSING DISORDER

In order to be classified as a disorder, problems with sensory processing must be both pervasive (occur in a variety of settings) and interfere with daily activity (or to be more technical, a major life activity, e.g., learning, walking, seeing, etc.). Sensory processing disorder includes three distinct patterns: sensory modulation disorder, sensory discrimination disorder, and sensory-based motor disorder. (Table 1 sums up the subtypes and hallmarks of these three.)

Table I: Sensory Processing Disorder		
Sensory Modulation Disorder (SMD)	*Sensory Discrimination Disorder (SDD)*	*Sensory-Based Motor Disorder (SBMD)*
Sensory Over-Responsivity *Ouch! Too bright! Fight-or-flight responses*	No subtypes—this child cannot differentiate different sensory aspects of objects appropriately	**Dyspraxia** *Lack of coordination, poor motor planning*
Sensory Under-Responsivity *Slumping, lethargic*		**Postural Disorder** *Poor posture*
Sensory-Seeking Craving *Biting, crashing, spinning*		

Sensory Modulation Disorder

A child with a *sensory modulation disorder* has difficulty interpreting and responding correctly to sensory information. The body may over-respond, under-respond, or vary in response to sensory information. For example, a child with sensory modulation disorder might interpret a haircut as an attack but crave spicy foods. The keys are that the brain doesn't interpret information correctly and the body responds in a way that is unequal to the sensory information coming in (Hanft, Miller, and Lane 2000). Sensory modulation disorder includes three subtypes: sensory over-responsivity, sensory under-responsivity, and sensory-seeking craving.

Sensory Over-Responsivity

A child with *sensory over-responsivity* is flooded with sensory input (noise, movement, touch, taste, smell), and thus easily overwhelmed. As a result, the child's body develops a protective response to this sensory information, leading to a fight-or-flight reaction. A child with sensory over-responsivity may scream hysterically when getting his nails trimmed. A light touch may feel like a slap.

Imagine what would happen if you were to open a jar of mayonnaise that has been in the refrigerator too long: you'd notice a smell, see mold growing, and—if you were foolish enough to taste it regardless—you would probably choke on it. To a child with over-responsive senses, common everyday foods can have the same effect. In these cases, the body's protective system is over-responsive, to the extent that it can be difficult to eat *anything* unless it's prepared according to that child's particular needs.

All children may display these or similar behaviors at one point or another. The aspects that make it a sensory processing disorder are that these behaviors are pervasive and significant enough to impact major life activities.

Sensory Under-Responsivity

Children with *sensory under-responsivity* have a protective response that is on holiday. They don't take in the information they need to learn about the world. These children often appear lethargic. Loud noise, bright lights, and hot surfaces may not bother them at all—in fact, they may not even notice! These children lack the ability to correctly interpret warnings from the environment. They may fail to recognize an oncoming car, or an angry dog. They may feel pain inappropriately and ignore a bleeding cut or a bump on the head.

When Under- and Over-Responsiveness Combine

A child can also be over-responsive in some areas and under-responsive in others. For example, Brendan has over-responsive senses of smell, sight, and hearing (he needs less sensory information in these areas)—things are often too bright, too loud, and too stinky to him. On the other hand, his senses of touch and taste are under-responsive (he needs more sensory information in those areas)—he has to squeeze, pinch, grab, hit, and bite in order to feel. This need becomes even more pronounced when he is stressed or otherwise overstimulated.

Sensory-Seeking Craving

You need to hold on to your hat to parent a child who is *sensory-seeking*. Remember the Tasmanian Devil—the cartoon character that spins around with a whirlwind of activity? The sensory-seeking child needs deep touch in order to feel. She may grab, pinch, bite, and hit, not out of maliciousness, but rather to obtain needed sensory input, and be able to interpret her world. She may spin, rock, or bounce in her seat. In contrast to the seemingly lethargic, undersensitive children, sensory-seeking children need constant bodily stimulation. For example, Aviva used to rub herself against the carpet while watching TV so much that it led to friction burns (Susan solved this problem by persuading Aviva to switch to a body massager).

In order to receive sensory input, a sensory-seeking child may also crave highly sweetened, salty, or spicy foods. Though Brendan detests spicy foods, he craves sweets. I've caught him on several occasions piling chairs on top of each other in order to reach a treasure of licorice, cookies, or anything else that is fortified with sugar. Brendan has also been known to provide himself with deep tactile and visual stimulation. For example, once, after a period of unusual quiet in our house, Brendan appeared at the top of the stairs, completely naked. Stamped all over his body were small, blue, round imprints of Spider-Man. As I picked my jaw up from the floor, he explained with great pride—and a loud growl—that he was a cheetah. In a very creative way, Brendan had provided himself with needed sensory input, all over his body.

Sensory Discrimination Disorder

A child with a *sensory discrimination disorder* has difficulty recognizing the different qualities or aspects of sensory information. For example, a child with sensory discrimination disorder might have difficulty distinguishing between a baseball and a tennis ball. I've seen a videotape of a girl assigned to find an object in a ball pit—she was clearly having fun but equally clearly having difficulty because she was unable to discriminate between the qualities of the object she was looking for and the qualities of the balls. While this may sound relatively benign, what if a child can't feel the sharp end of a knife in a drawer of silverware? Remember: children learn everything about the world around them through their senses.

Sensory-Based Motor Disorder

A child with a *sensory-based motor disorder* may have difficulty sequencing new motor actions. Think of the skills involved in a relatively simple game like soccer. To play soccer a child must filter out all other surrounding activity, determine the boundaries in which the game is played, and identify what to do with that ball. Once the child actually reaches the ball, a kick must then be orchestrated—which involves the coordination of lots of muscles. A child with a sensory-based motor disorder may have difficulty not just learning team sports, but also writing, running, jumping, catching, throwing, typing—or even just sitting up. There are two types of sensory-based motor disorder: dyspraxia and postural disorder.

Dyspraxia

The term "praxis" refers to the ability to plan motor events. Ayres defined *praxis* as the ability to plan, organize, and execute new motor tasks such as typing, skiing, and learning to play an instrument (Lane, Miller, and Hanft 2000). A child who has *dyspraxia*—dysfunctional praxis—has difficulty imagining, coordinating, and realizing unfamiliar movements.

Postural Disorder

Children with *postural disorder* may have difficulty sitting up, attending to tasks, and "organizing" their bodies—this is the child who practically lies on top of the desk when writing.

FINE-TUNING THE SPD DIAGNOSIS

It can be difficult to understand the different aspects of your child's behavior. Research shows that children with SPD often have overlapping disorders (Miller et al. 2001; Miller et al. 1999; Wang, Wang, and Ren 2003). What is unclear at this point is whether SPD is a true disorder on its own, or whether it exists only as a component of other disorders. This can make treatment difficult. Take Brendan for example. When we were trying to understand his disorder, it was unclear which came first, ADHD or SPD. Sometimes it feels as though we're trying to juggle different disorders, each with different characteristics. Which do we prioritize? And how should we explain his needs? When I rattle off that Brendan has ADHD and SPD people tend to look at me as if I'm nuts.

SPD and the Brain

Research suggests that children with SPD (and other disorders) may actually be physiologically different (Miller et al. 2001). Thus, SPD may always be present, even when your child is an adult. Your child needs to recognize the impact of SPD and learn lifelong coping strategies.

Early intervention is critical in the treatment of children with SPD, so that the children can learn to successfully cope with their differences. Also, it's important to remember that SPD commonly appears with many other disorders, including autism, ADHD, fragile X, cerebral palsy, and mental retardation to name a few. This means that your child's diagnosis may in fact appear blurry to you and to the professionals who provide care, making it even more challenging to identify the components of SPD and provide appropriate treatment.

While there may in fact be some structural differences in the way your child processes information, as with any disorder, some children will be only mildly impacted, while others are more seriously affected. My daughter Lauren has what I consider to be a mild form of sensory issues. At the age of eight, she's still constantly using her fingers to eat—spaghetti, lasagna, anything. She also loves salty and spicy foods, and frequently twirls from one place to the other. While this may tap my patience, in the grand scheme of things her behaviors, while irritating, don't seriously impact any of her major life activities: she functions well in school and has lots of friends.

Mixed Diagnoses: SPD and Other Disorders and Complications

In this section, we'll look at how characteristics of SPD overlap with other disorders and complications, and then talk about treatment. I will provide you with some basic background information about each specific disorder and complication, but keep in mind that the purpose here is to help you identify the characteristics and functioning of your child, not to provide a clinical diagnosis.

Autism.   This past fourth of July weekend my wife took the children on a trip so that I would have time to write. On the evening of the fourth, my father and I went to see the fireworks in Boulder, Colorado. Completely by chance we ran into my older brother Roger. He was impeccably dressed in coat and tie. (If you've ever been to Boulder in the summer—or any time of the year for that matter—you'll know he was a bit out of place in this attire.) At any rate, as we watched the fireworks, Roger gritted his teeth and rocked back and forth.

With your understanding of SPD, you'll recognize that Roger was providing himself with vestibular and proprioceptive sensation. Roger has displayed autistic behaviors since he was a child; when we were young I remember my brother frequently rocking back and forth, gritting his teeth, and occasionally sucking air deeply into his chest, and then exhaling. As I watched him this evening, it was clear that he was enthralled; it was as if he were seeing fireworks for the first time. Thinking of Brendan, I felt connected; I understood where he was coming from.

So what is autism? The Individuals with Disabilities Education Act (IDEA) of 2004 identifies three characteristics of autism: a limited range of social interactions, impaired communication skills, and a persistent pattern of stereotypical behaviors, activities, and interests. According to the *Diagnostic and Statistical Manual of Mental Disorders* (DSM-IV), autism is a spectrum disorder which includes autistic disorder, Rett's disorder, childhood disintegrative disorder, Asperger's syndrome, and pervasive developmental disorder. Essentially, this means that children can look and function very differently within the autism spectrum. Some children with autism are nonverbal while others ramble on and on. What is common, however, is a marked difference in the way children with autism interact with others and with their environment.

Children with autism often display characteristics of SPD. One study found that motion sensitivity was significantly decreased in children with autism when compared to their peers, leading researchers to conclude that children with autism have less efficient visual-perceptual processing abilities (Bertone et al. 2003). And finally, a study conducted at the STAR Center found that children with autism—like children with SPD—have significantly different reactions to sensory information than typical peers (Miller et al. 2001).

ADHD.   Five years ago, I was the special education coordinator at a charter school run by a for-profit company. People toured the school so frequently that it just became part of the day. One day, as I was walking a child with severe ADHD back to his class ("walking" is perhaps the wrong word—he never walked, he twirled), we both observed an older gentleman ahead of us touring with the principal and the child's teacher. Without a moment's hesitation, the child ran up ahead, jumped on the back of the gentleman, grabbed his toupee, and exuberantly shouted "Hi" to his teacher. I stood with my mouth agape. No one said anything. The older gentleman, beet red, took his hairpiece from the child and put it back in place. He turned out to be the company's vice president.

Though this is an extreme example of sensory-seeking behavior, children with ADHD frequently display characteristics of SPD. According to Goldman et al. (1998), ADHD accounts for "approximately half of all pediatric referrals to mental health services in the United States." And over half of these children diagnosed with ADHD present other psychological/behavioral disorders, including anxiety and depression. (Nevertheless, many children with ADHD perform extremely well in school, and are able to tap into the energy and creativity associated with the disorder.)

Multiple studies suggest that children with ADHD may have symptoms or characteristics of SPD. A study that compared balance function of children with ADHD to that of typical children found that children with ADHD demonstrated poor stability and abnormal sensory integration—and the researchers went so far as to suggest that there might be a link between balance instability and other symptoms of cognition and behavior (Wang, Wang, and Ren 2003). Another study, this one exploring the link between tactile sensitivity and ADHD, found a significant difference between children with ADHD and typical children in completing tactile tasks (Parush et al. 1997).

Premature birth.   Studies suggest that 30 percent to 50 percent of all children born prematurely will have a neurological disorder such as SPD or ADHD. Susan, my coauthor, gave birth to Aviva at twenty-four weeks, instead of the usual forty weeks.

Two excellent books about preemies and the challenges parents of preemies face are *Alex: The Fathering of a Preemie* by Jeff Stimpson, and *Parenting Your Premature Baby and Child* by Mara Tesler Stein and Deborah Davis. The former is written from the perspective of a father, and the latter offers a comprehensive overview of issues facing preemies and parents of preemies, including family, couple, and relationship issues.

Learning disabilities.   Studies suggest that approximately 70 percent of children with learning disabilities also have sensory issues. For these children, therapy should address the underlying difficulties in processing sensations rather than just symptoms of inattention. Unfortunately, until recently many doctors and teachers assumed these children had ADHD in conjunction with a learning disability. Fuller evaluations—including an assessment by an occupational therapist—can lead to a correct diagnosis.

TREATMENT

All of my memories of childhood summers are of playing in sprinklers, eating outside, and running around barefoot just about every day, so it's important to me as a father to have a decent yard. For the past three years, however, a fungus has plagued my lawn. This year, I got so frustrated that I took a sample of grass to the lawn doctor at a small independent nursery; she informed me that I could never get rid of it. Apparently a fungus is an opportunist that takes over when a lawn is unhealthy. Instead of prescribing more fungicide, she instructed me to develop the natural health of the lawn by watering deeply, aerating, and using organic materials.

For me, this is a great analogy to how to treat SPD. Like the fungus, SPD is something of an opportunist; it will never go away. Thus, for treatment, the majority of our efforts should be on developing the natural health of our child. While there may be a role for medicine (fungicide), it shouldn't be the primary focus.

How, then, can we build the natural health of our child? Basically, what's good for all children is good for children with SPD—perhaps even more so. Exercise, good nutrition, time spent in nature, and, of course, love, are critical to the overall health and well-being of a child. Of course, there are many other elements to a child's well-being, including a strong family, good health care, adequate housing, and a safe community. However, since control of these elements is often out of our hands, let's focus on the first three elements.

Exercise and Nutrition

Of course, exercise and nutrition benefit all children, but perhaps especially children with SPD or overlapping disorders. In one study, researchers found that after exercise, children with autism performed better in the classroom and self-stimulatory behaviors decreased (Rosenthal-Malek and Mitchell 1997). One good way to encourage children to exercise—and to eat a healthy diet and spend time in nature—is through modeling. Children want to be like their parents; by taking care of yourself, you'll inspire your child to do so, too.

Diets as treatments are definitely controversial. I believe you should do your best to feed your child nutritious foods, free of empty calories. If this becomes a challenge to the extent that your child's health is impaired, contact your child's doctor.

Nature

In Last Child in the Woods: Saving Our Children from Nature-Deficit Disorder (2005), Richard Louv suggests that spending time in nature leads to many benefits, including increased abilities to problem solve, think critically, and make decisions. Spending time in nature can also help alleviate symptoms of depression, obesity, and ADHD. Moreover, research suggests that interaction with nature can even increase children's self-esteem and emotional development, as well as lead to a reduction in aggressive behaviors (Feral 1999).

THE ROLE OF OCCUPATIONAL THERAPY

Currently, occupational therapy is the primary treatment for SPD. In occupational therapy, children with SPD learn to understand the sensations they're feeling and how to manage them. In the following boxed text, occupational therapist Bridget Bax describes both how occupational therapists work with children with SPD and how to obtain an evaluation for SPD.

There are two main models of occupational therapy. If your child receives occupational therapy in the school, she's going to receive an *educational model* of services, one that concentrates on how a child learns. The focus here will be on education and adapting the environment or instruction so that it is more meaningful for the child. If your child receives occupational therapy in a clinic setting, he's going to receive a *medical model* of services, one that's disease- or disorder-based. The focus here will be on improving a child's ability to take care of himself in daily tasks.

Also, different occupational therapists may advocate for different treatment approaches, including hippotherapy (occupational therapy on a horse), aquatherapy, and craniosacral therapy. What's important is that the therapist is certified, has a solid background in sensory integration theory, and has worked successfully with other children with SPD.

Some aspects of occupational therapy benefit children in general, not just children with SPD. Virtually every occupational therapist I've worked with has encouraged me to use therapy balls as seats for my students regardless of their diagnosis or needs. Research has found that the use of therapy balls in the classroom increases in-seat behavior and writing legibility with all students who used them, not just those with ADHD (Schilling and Schwartz 2003). In my experience, therapy balls tend to be popular with most of my students, not just those with SPD or ADHD.

The Role of Therapy in the Treatment of Children with Sensory Processing Disorder

Occupations are the activities of everyday life which hold meaning for either an individual or the culture. An occupational therapist helps people with differing abilities to attain, regain, and maintain the important and meaningful skills of everyday life.

SPD typically interferes with a child's ability to participate in meaningful occupations. Common occupations of childhood include: playing, self-care skills, school-related tasks, social skills, and chores. It's the occupational therapist's role to address sensory processing problems as they relate to a child's ability to do these activities.

Sensory processing problems can make it hard for a child in many ways. For example, a child who is tactile defensive may avoid social situations out of fear of being touched. A child who has difficulty modulating sensory input may have attention difficulties at school or be unable to complete routines without getting distracted. A child who doesn't process sensory input appropriately may lack adequate motor coordination and thus not try playground equipment out of fear of failure. Occupational therapists directly address these sensory processing challenges so that children with SPD can more successfully participate in the important tasks (occupations) of their daily life.

If parents are concerned that their child has SPD, they should contact their primary care physician and inquire about an occupational therapy evaluation. An occupational therapy evaluation should include both a thorough parent interview and clinical evaluations. Assessment with standardized tests is valuable if the child is cognitively and behaviorally able to participate in such tests with reliable results. Common standardized assessments used during an occupational therapy evaluation include the Sensory Integration and Praxis Test (SIPT), the Miller Assessment for Preschoolers, the Bruininks-Oseretsky Test of Motor Proficiency, the Peabody

Developmental Motor Scales, the DeGangi Burke, and a form of the Sensory Profile. (Typically only one or two of the above-mentioned standardized assessments are administered.)

An occupational therapy evaluation doesn't, however, lead to a diagnosis from an occupational therapist for two reasons:

1. Occupational therapists do not diagnose; only a physician can provide a diagnosis.

2. There's no diagnostic code specific to SPD. Occupational therapists using a sensory integration treatment approach see children with a variety of diagnoses, including lack of coordination, encephalopathy, autism spectrum or pervasive developmental disorder (PDD), unspecified disorder of the autonomic nervous system, and disturbance of tactile sensation.

Insurance companies and Medicaid will normally provide for at least some occupational therapy if it's deemed medically necessary because the child isn't able to perform normal activities.

When choosing a therapy provider to address a child's occupational performance needs as they relate to SPD, it's important that the therapist has received a bachelor's degree or higher level degree in occupational therapy. It's equally important that the therapist have postgraduate or continuing education classes related to sensory integration (theory and treatment) and sensory processing disorders. If a therapist is administering the Sensory Integration and Praxis Test (SIPT), they must be SIPT certified. Parents should not be afraid to ask for a potential therapist's résumé or examples of specific training the therapist has undertaken.

(See the resources section at the back of this book to find more information on how to find qualified OTs.)

  —Bridget E. Bax, OTR
  Board member, The KID Foundation
  Occupational Therapist, The Children's Hospital, Denver

FINAL THOUGHTS

After reading this chapter, you should now understand the basic concepts of SPD and the three different patterns of SPD: sensory modulation disorder, sensory discrimination disorder, and sensory-based motor disorder. Remember, too, that SPD frequently overlaps with other disorders, including ADHD, autism, mental retardation, learning disabilities, and fragile X; some children born prematurely may also display SPD.

In terms of treatment, children with SPD may need specific therapy in order to perform everyday activities; occupational therapy is currently the primary treatment for SPD. Also, children with SPD can benefit from what is beneficial to all children—exercise, good nutrition, and time spent in nature.

The next chapter will begin to teach you the strategies and skills to strengthen your family. Remember: a child with SPD will have a much better quality of life in a family with strong relationships, supportive siblings, involved fathers, and a strong cultural identity.

Chapter 2

SPD Is a Family Affair

Go to the Mosquito Thou Dejected

Screens on the windows and netted bed,
Still the mosquitoes surround my head.
Queer to me how they can find a hole,
Force their way through and scent their goal.

Cellar door, kitchen door, roof skylight,
Up the net, down the net, all the night,
Cheering each other with busy hum
Till at last, woe is me, through they come.

When you feel hampered by hindrance met,
Hindrance with meshes as fine as net,
Keep your buzzing and you'll get through
Just as persistent mosquitoes do.

—Frederick S. Miller

Frederick S. Miller was my great-grandfather. He wrote this poem—
and many others—while serving as a missionary in Korea for forty-five
years. This chapter is dedicated to him, in honor of the family traditions of service, education, and strong family relationships he estab-
lished. Growing up, my brothers and I loved to hear the stories my
grandmother and great-aunt shared of their lives in the Far East during
the early 1900s.

What does this have to do with SPD? First, just as the mosquitoes
in my great-grandfather's poem are persistent, it takes persistence to
raise a child with SPD. There are many obstacles and challenges to
doing so that only a member of the SPD community can fully understand. Second, one of the great strengths of a family can be its connection to a rich history. Our history has certainly helped define my
family's values and purpose.

THE EMOTIONAL JOURNEY

The emotional challenges of raising a child with a disability can be
overwhelming and isolating. In the mid-1960s, a psychiatrist recommended that my brother Roger be placed in the state institution
because at the age of five he still had only limited verbal ability and
was very aggressive. While my parents had the strength to disagree,
they also often felt alone against the world. Relatives and family
acquaintances didn't understand my brother's needs and often found
fault with my mother. (It was widely believed at the time that the
socially withdrawn characteristics of autism were the result of a lack of
maternal nurturing.) Not surprisingly, my parents experienced a lot of
different, intense emotions about the situation.

This is common; typical emotional responses to having a child
with a disability include initial denial, anger, grief, fear, guilt, confu-
sion, disappointment, and rejection (Kupper 1993). Individuals cycle
through these emotions to a place of acceptance at different rates. This
is important to understand in your relationships with others. For example, relatives who don't spend as much time with your child may take
longer to understand your child's behavior and move more slowly
through the different feelings. Knowing others with disabilities—or

having had positive or negative experiences with other people with disabilities—can also play an important role in a person's process through this emotional journey.

Transition events—including starting kindergarten, changing schools, participation in team sports, puberty, and the onset of dating—can also trigger the emotional cycle anew. Significant transition events can be linked to unexpressed expectations; when reality is more difficult, or even just different than what's expected, it's natural to feel disappointed, angry, etc.

For example, Brendan started playing soccer this fall. While I didn't think I had any preconceived expectations for his performance, it was sometimes difficult to watch him play. His deficits were apparent. He clearly didn't understand the game and was frustrated by his own lack of coordination. On several occasions he became aggressive and hit other players—hard. It felt as though every parent on the soccer field must be wondering what was wrong with this devil child and judging both of us. How could I make them understand how Brendan must feel to be so challenged by something all the other kids found so easy? Did they think I was just an incompetent parent?

A Change of Focus

Doubt in your abilities as a parent comes at a high emotional cost. Add in the monetary expense of raising a child with special needs—buying books, special materials, co-pays, professional expenses, medication, etc. And, too, all of the extra costs; for example, broken windows, broken glasses, carpets covered in ink, and clothing torn to shreds. All of this can easily impact your relationship with your partner and your friendships, which then also puts additional stresses on your other children. Before you know it, it may feel as though your family is controlled by SPD!

Leadership and inspirational programs teach that we go toward our focus. Our focus creates a self-fulfilling prophecy: If we focus on problems with our family, our children, or our spouses, these problems become greater. However, if we focus on solutions and strengths, these elements become stronger.

ACTIVITY: DEVELOPING A POSITIVE FOCUS

Here's one way to develop a positive focus: keep a record of the strengths of both your child and your family through photos, movies, journaling, a portfolio, or whatever suits your style. A colleague of mine makes quilts as a way of telling her family's story. Scrapbooking is another good alternative that's easier than ever these days with supplies available everywhere. On bad days, revisiting your record of the good times can help you refocus on the important things.

My father keeps joking that these are the good years of parenting—even when Brendan broke my glasses in a restaurant. I keep telling him that I'm still waiting. He's right, though. Amidst all of the challenges of raising a child with SPD, there are also wonderful discoveries of strengths—in Brendan, the rest of the family, and ourselves.

The next section focuses on some of these challenges families face. Remember, the goal here is to move toward a positive focus; to use the challenges of raising a child with SPD to become a better parent and build a stronger family.

CHALLENGES TO THE FAMILY

Forming and maintaining a healthy family is always challenging, even for families without children with special needs. In a study conducted by the YMCA of the United States and the Search Institute (Roehlkepartain et al. 2002), parents identified the following factors as challenges to effective parenting:

- Job demands (50 percent)

- Sibling rivalry (48 percent)

- Overscheduling (41 percent)

- Family finances (41 percent)

- Pressure to buy things (34 percent)

- Being single/low support (24 percent)

When parents were asked what could make the task of parenting easier, they identified the following factors as useful supports to effective parenting:

- Talking with other parents (81 percent)

- Advice from trusted professionals (76 percent)

- Trusted adults spending time with their children (71 percent)

Researchers in Australia, Canada, and Israel have also identified nine quality of life areas specific to families with children with disabilities which have been found to be important for family health and well-being. These nine areas are:

1. Health

2. Financial well-being

3. Family relationships

4. Support from others

5. Support from disability-related services

6. Spiritual and cultural beliefs

7. Careers

8. Leisure and enjoyment of life

9. Community and civic involvement

THE OPPORTUNITY

If we truly believe in people's strengths, we'll see people as a measure of their characters—how far they have come, not where they are at. The opportunity here, then, is to reframe how your family views SPD, so that SPD becomes an opportunity to bring out your true character and the character of your family. Living with SPD isn't easy. It can be *easier*, however, if it's viewed as an opportunity to create a stronger family and a deeper, richer life.

Reframe How You Think About SPD

Any stressful event is an opportunity to strengthen your character and the character of your family. As a parent, the challenges of SPD have the possibility of bringing out your best qualities. You can be an example for your children. Undoubtedly they, too, will face challenging circumstances in their lives, but you can teach them through example how to respond positively and grow from challenges.

Research has found that people who respond positively to stressful events exhibit specific behavior patterns: they tend to search for the meaning or cause of the stress, seek to gain control over the situation, look for positive aspects of the situation, and compare themselves favorably to others dealing with similar circumstances (Summers, Behr, and Turnbull 1988).

Other studies have also found that the challenges of raising a child with special needs can actually lead to a closer family, personal growth, and greater appreciation for the simple things in life. Parents often also learn patience, unselfishness, and compassion from raising a child with special needs. This book is intended to help you nurture these attitudes.

Personal Reflection

Think about the challenges your child brings to your family.

What issues have been particularly difficult? (Refer back to the list of challenges to effective parenting earlier in this chapter for ideas.)

Now think about what you've gained from your child. Do you have a new appreciation now of the support you receive from family members or friends? Of the ability of your child to grow and learn? Of your relationships?

How have you changed as a result of these experiences?

Another Family's Experience

The following story demonstrates the growth and self-realization possible with acceptance of a disability. While the story focuses on becoming a parent-leader, read it with an awareness of the challenges

Evan's Story

My son, Evan, is an extraordinary young man. At age ten, he has such personality and charisma that all who come in contact with Evan adore him. Evan was diagnosed with ADHD when he was eight. I immediately read everything I could get my hands on about it in order to help him. I was diagnosed with ADHD a few months later. Shortly after my diagnosis, Evan was further diagnosed as having anxiety and sensory processing disorders.

Meeting the needs of Evan and our family has been difficult. It still proves difficult! Each of Evan's three conditions also has coexisting conditions, which many times present the same (or similar) symptoms. I wonder if there is yet something else going on. It seems so never-ending sometimes! We try to take things day by day.

Even with all the books and information out there, it still comes down to us all being individuals. Just because one child with ADHD reacts to therapy in a certain way doesn't mean that another will react the same. The same goes for SPD, anxiety, etc. It can be so frustrating. We want the best for our kids but when is it too much? When is it too little? You finally get your child's medications titrated and then *boom!*—you wake up one morning and they no longer work and you're back to square one. But that's the way life is; it was never meant to be easy. It's precisely these challenges that make us better, stronger people. It's because of the conditions Evan has that he's the extraordinary human being he is. I would not change that for the world.

—*Susan P. Simpson*
Mother and parent advocate

this family has overcome and the resulting growth it has achieved. This mother, also named Susan and also with a son named Evan, clearly has an appreciation for her child's strengths as well as an acceptance of her child's disability.

TAKING CARE OF YOUR FAMILY

While you may not have actually signed up for the task, if you're a parent, you're also a leader. Susan, Evan's mother, described her experience of becoming a parent-leader like this:

> *It's difficult to really explain how one becomes a parent-leader. For me, there was no real turning point to speak of, it just evolved that way. After all the phone calls, the research, the books, the workshops, etc., I began to see that the only person who could truly advocate for my son was (and is) me. That's not to say that there aren't others out there to help, because there most certainly are—it's just to say that nobody knows your child better than you. Even though I am constantly advocating for Evan, I am now also at a place where I can help others advocate for their children. I have been able to grow beyond just looking at my son and his needs. Now I can look towards others and help them with their children. This is gratifying beyond words. Giving back—that's what it's all about.*

Leadership Styles

What, you may be wondering, does being a leader have to do with having a child with SPD? As the parent of a child with SPD, you'll have to be a leader in some special ways. For example, you may have to help your own family learn to cope with your child's behavior. Or you may have to guide your child's school in providing appropriate supports and services. Or you may choose to help other parents, as Susan describes above. Leaders come in a variety of styles:

The Charismatic Style

The outgoing, charismatic style is most commonly associated with leadership. President Clinton was this kind of leader. He was able to work a crowd with finesse, using charm to persuade others to support his initiatives. This leadership style can be very effective for managing behavior. In the home, the charismatic style might be used to redirect your children to another activity, or "sell" a task to them. To use this style, first connect with your child, so that he believes that you understand his needs. Next, build up what it is that you want your child to do, sincerely but persuasively. Finally, praise your child, sincerely and specifically.

The Inspirational Style

The inspirational style is most commonly associated with church pastors and civil rights leaders. This leader inspires followers to take up the cause. Inspiration can be used to motivate your children; this works best when you involve your child's ideas, and tap into her enthusiasms. For example, you might use inspiration to focus your child on doing well in school. You could start by asking her for her ideas on what would help her work in school. Help her identify what excites her and what would help her get more done. If she's interested in animals, get books on animals that she can have as rewards for completing schoolwork. Let her teachers know about her interests, so that these can be used in the classroom, both to study the topic (writing assignments can be done just as easily about lemurs as about what I did this summer) and as rewards (e.g., a child could spend time with a favorite book after finishing a math assignment).

The Intellectual Style

Intellectual leaders encourage problem solving and diverse thinking. The poet Maya Angelou might fall under this style of leadership, having become a leader by encouraging others to solve societal problems in her role as an activist. In the home, you might use an intellectual style to encourage siblings to work out their conflicts on their own. Or you might use this style to promote greater independence in your children. Help your child identify appropriate solutions to problems not by thinking for him, but by asking questions and getting him to come up with solutions.

Personal Reflection

Think about your personal leadership style. As a parent-leader, you're teaching your children in a number of important ways: you're teaching them how to be responsible for their own lives, how to manage their own daily activities and tasks now as children, and how to be responsible adults.

Which of these different styles do you identify with most? Your choice of style offers insights into how you tend to address challenges and behavior.

Do you tend to persuade your children (charismatic), or do you tend to explain why things should be done in a certain way (intellectual)?

Most likely you use all of these styles at different times. In which situations do you use which style? Is that style effective? Is there another style that might work better?

Having read these descriptions of different styles, is there another style you might like to try?

Transformational Leadership

Transformational leaders effect lasting change by taking leadership styles to a higher level. The transformational leader sets the values for good character, establishes clear standards, and motivates a child to reach her fullest potential by encouraging autonomy (the ability to do things for yourself).

These are skills common to all effective parents. The challenge of being a parent of a child with SPD is that these skills become even more important. You may have to be a stronger transformational leader than other parents you know because it can be more difficult for your child to take risks and self-manage. Furthermore, behaviors that may be cute in a preschool child with SPD can become very serious problems in a teenager.

By setting clear standards and encouraging autonomy, you'll create a stronger family. While you may not realize it, you may also find yourself becoming more confident and assertive. These skills can even help in your work environment. You might also begin to understand how to communicate better with your partner. What you create in your home can even serve as motivation for other families you know to recognize and support special needs in their children. At this point, you don't know how far-reaching the possibilities are for becoming a stronger, more transformational person.

Personal Reflection

What does becoming an even more effective transformational leader mean to you? How would that benefit your family?

How do you demonstrate values in your family?

How do you set clear standards?

How do you encourage your kids to do things for themselves?

How do you encourage risk taking?

Do your family members support a culture that encourages autonomy, risk taking, and reaching one's fullest potential?

What resources or information do you need to become an even more effective transformational leader?

Look Beyond Appearances

Maria's parents were both migrant farm workers in California. Her mother Anna had a second-grade education; her father didn't have any formal schooling at all.

When Maria was a child she was made to sit outside the classroom for some infraction (now long since forgotten). When Anna learned this, she became irate. In her opinion, Maria's job was to be at school, to study and learn. If Maria was sitting outside of the classroom, how could she possibly be doing this?

Dressed all in clothes from the Salvation Army, Anna walked her daughter to school and asked to meet with her teacher. Anna didn't speak any English, so Maria had to translate her angry words. Through Maria, Anna insisted that Maria remain in the classroom at all times. Anna's determination that Maria get a good education left a lasting impression on Maria (and undoubtedly on the school staff, too). Maria earned a scholarship to Harvard; she's currently on the board of trustees of another respected university, and in her career reports directly to a mayor.

Was Maria's mother perfect? I don't know anything more about her, but I doubt it. Was she a leader? Absolutely. She was a leader through her actions. Though she had little education herself, her actions clearly taught Maria the value of education.

Identifying a Role Model

Great people—and great parents—are always striving to become better. That's one of the characteristics of the transformational leader. In striving to become a better parent, you also model to your children that self-growth is a lifelong process.

To become an even more effective parent, it can help to model a parent you admire. For example, you might appreciate your neighbor's ability to balance work and family. Or maybe you have a cousin who has extremely well-mannered children, or an aunt who was a second mother to you. It's okay to go back into your own childhood and think of the adults that you knew then. Who stands out?

Use this person as a model to work toward. (Your model doesn't have to be living or real—feel free to create your model from memory or imagination.) Regardless of how you come to your model parent, your model should be clear and concrete in your mind. It can help to think of a smell or feel you associate with this person; for example, you might remember the smell of your grandmother's kitchen, or your happiness at your grandfather's laughter.

Remember: while it's important to acknowledge your weaknesses, it's also important to focus on how you want to improve and what that might look like.

Personal Reflection

How would you feel if your model were sitting in the room with you? How would others feel? Would you feel safe or secure? Would you want to laugh or smile?

What does your model do to make you and others feel this way?

How do children act in the same room with this person? Why?

How do your children act when you are in the room? Why?

What do you most admire about your model?

What do other people admire about you?

What would be the benefit of being more like your model?

What legacy is your model leaving for his or her children?

What legacy do you want to leave for your children? How do you want them to remember you?

ACTIVITY: THE PARENT-LEADER

As you think about the above questions, formulate one goal to help you become more like this parent you want to be. Make your goal big and broad. Make it capture the essence of who you want to become. When you've developed your goal, write it down where you can see it every day. Include any pictures or drawings that will help you focus on your goal.

Next, think of three measurable steps that you could take over the next six months that would get you closer to who you want to become. For example, if your goal is to recognize and appreciate the strengths of your child, your three steps might be:

1. Create a bulletin board somewhere in your house and ask your child to post what he thinks is his best work of the week on it.

2. Include a note in your child's lunch every Friday about what has been his most significant contribution to the family that week.

3.   Set aside an hour every weekend to engage in any activity of your child's choosing (budget permitting).

As you work on your self-development, monitor your progress. Set aside time in your calendar for reflection on your progress at the end or beginning of every month. During this time, ask yourself the following questions:

Have I been consistently using the three steps I identified?

Are these steps helping me to become more like my model parent?

Do I need to change any of the three steps?

Have there been any differences in my parenting? Do I have information from other sources (children, friends, partner, relatives, etc.) to support this?

Why do I want to become like my model parent? What is the value to me, to my family, and to my child?

When you've been consistently working toward your goal, celebrate! Plan a reward for yourself that fits into your budget and time.

TAKING CARE OF YOURSELF

Lots of areas in your life can also cause stress. Work can be one source of stress, as can depression, financial anxieties, and conflict with a partner or close relative. You may also have feelings of guilt, anger, and sorrow about the diagnosis of SPD itself.

Whatever the source of these emotions, it's critical that you take care of yourself. If your depression isn't managed well, you have to work long hours, or your physical health isn't taken care of, it can be difficult to take good care of your family.

Taking care of yourself means eating well, getting appropriate exercise, and having regular physical exams. It also means taking some time to yourself every week. It's impossible to be on duty 24/7 and still expect to be an effective parent. Everyone needs a break to refuel and recharge. Friends are important, too. It's easy to get so absorbed in your family and the needs of your children that you neglect your friends, but friendships are invaluable. Even though I rarely see my oldest friends, it's still comforting, even at my age, to know that they're out there. Old friends can be like additional relatives for your children.

Personal Reflection

What emotions get in the way of your ability to be the best parent you can be? Do you get so angry or frustrated that you feel you make bad decisions about parenting? Are you aware of these feelings and what's behind them? Do you have a plan to deal with these issues? Have you considered talking with a close friend or your partner, or do you need professional help?

Do you take care of your physical health? If so, how? If not, make a plan to take care of yourself.

Do you have close relationships? How many friends could you call and ask for help? Do you feel satisfied with this network? What can you do to find friends who will be there for you? Do you have time to yourself and time with friends each week? If not, schedule this time into your week.

What resources do you need to take better care of yourself so that you can be the best parent you can be?

In chapter 8 we'll talk more about how to handle stress; you may want to refer back to your answers to this personal reflection then.

FINAL THOUGHTS

Having a child with SPD can raise a host of emotions; these can impact you at different times in the life of your child and your family. It's important to understand both that you're not alone in feeling these emotions and that they occur in a cycle which eventually ends in a period of acceptance. This cycle can also begin anew during key transition periods such as starting school, participating in team sports, and dating.

While SPD brings many challenges to your family, it can also be an opportunity for the almost unlimited growth of yourself, your family, and your children. Think about what you can achieve: a stronger, closer family and a greater appreciation for the simple things in life.

As a parent, you're also a leader; you demonstrate leadership skills every day. As the parent of a child with SPD, you may need to become an even more effective leader. Enhanced leadership skills can also transfer to work and relationships.

To end as we began, the following poem by my great-grandfather describes the importance of appreciating the simple things in life:

Sanctified Near-Sightedness

The fruit that hangs too near to me
Is oft the fruit I fail to see;
Though best and sweetest it may be
I leave it hanging on the tree.

I know so many who demand
Some special blessing, rare and grand,
Who, searching far o'er sea and land,
Neglect the mercies near at hand.

Some wish they could enjoy life more,
And fail to romp upon the floor
With chubby cherubs, three or four,
As sweet as mother ever bore.

And some, Herculean tasks would seek,
Ascend some ice-clad Alpine peak,
When 'tis far harder to be meek
Or stay at home and help the weak.
Whene'er your seeking lacks success,
Your telescopic eye confess
And ask the Lord your soul to bless
With sanctified near-sightedness.

—Frederick S. Miller

Chapter 3

Strengthening Relationships

When your child first gets diagnosed—whatever that diagnosis may be—it's easy to get totally caught up in what your child needs. Appointments get scheduled; medications and diet are carefully planned. Meetings with teachers and special educators take up a lot of your time. If your child needs help with dressing, eating, or toileting, time and energy are spent on these daily tasks, too. Even your budget gets affected—therapy, special equipment, etc. all add up.

So far, we've talked about what SPD is and how to live with a child with SPD. Now we'll focus on a relationship that can be the source of all the strength and resources you need to help your family—your marriage. (If you aren't married to the other parent of your child, please work on the issues with your partner. If you are in a relationship with someone else, work with that person as well. The stronger all your intimate relationships are, the better off your whole family will be.)

This chapter is a little different from the others in the book. It's written directly by me, Susan, using my professional expertise and my personal experiences to share some ideas about strengthening relationships. Strengthening relationships is something I've been interested in for a long time. Not only have I cowritten six books on the topic, I've also witnessed firsthand the difference a strong marriage can make in a child's life.

THE FAMILY SYSTEM

A family is like any other biological system: it seeks to establish a stable equilibrium where everyone in the family plays a role—and then tries to stay there. Kids go to school, parents work, housework gets done in spare moments. Changes upset the system. If Mom gets the flu, the schedule gets messed up. If Dad gets laid off, Mom has to go back to work or take a second job. If a child is born, the marital relationship is changed forever.

The desire of any organism to keep things the same is called *homeostasis*. It's true of our cells, our bodies, our families, and our society. When tornados or hurricanes hit, communities rush to bring things back to normal. But to return to normal, every change must be appropriately balanced. For example, if you eat too many bananas, you'll need more fiber to bring your system back into balance. This need for balance happens in our relationships as well.

Our Family's Story

When I went into labor with my first child just twenty-four weeks into my pregnancy, my life turned upside down. I was only six months pregnant. I'd only just started to wear maternity clothes and suddenly I wasn't pregnant anymore—I had a one-pound-eleven-ounce baby fighting for her life in a neonatal intensive care unit (NICU). Instead of buying blankets and diapers, my husband Lewis and I spent hours every day in the hospital. We sat beside our baby's isolette unit, watching her breathing on the ventilator, watching her being fed by IV. Her eyes opened for the first time when she was nine days old. The following day her lungs burst from the pressure of the ventilator. She needed emergency surgery to insert chest tubes to relieve the pressure of the air on her heart. We placed a do not resuscitate (DNR) order on her the next day, believing that if her heart gave out, she needed to be allowed to go. After three weeks, her lungs healed, and the DNR was lifted. We were finally allowed to hold our child when she was nearly a month old.

As you can imagine, the shock to our family system was overwhelming. Our expectations for what having a baby would be like were totally turned upside down; we had very little energy for each other. We didn't know how to regain our balance.

When Aviva came home from the hospital the shocks continued. She weighed only four pounds, five ounces, and was on an apnea monitor to alert us if she stopped breathing. She didn't sit up, roll over, or put her toes in her mouth—though she did smile and coo, and loved to bat at balls and toys in the air. She started occupational and physical therapy when she was eleven months old. She got her first pair of glasses at twelve months, after we found she had very little vision in one eye; she pulled to a stand for the very first time the next day. After two months of intensive therapy, she crawled; she first walked when she was seventeen months old, after several more months of therapy. She had no words, however; at eighteen months she still didn't even imitate sounds.

Our family was finally given a diagnosis of SPD when Aviva was two years old. Aviva required intense stimulation—brushing, massage, holding. She couldn't sleep unless she was physically touching one of us, lying full length on our bodies as we rocked her to sleep. And although she loved her therapy, my husband and I also spent time every day working on her skills and finding new ways to help her—music therapy, Gymboree classes, play groups run by physical therapists, etc.

So, what happened to our marriage? We had certain advantages—by the time Aviva was born we had been together twenty years, and married for more than eleven. We were older parents; I was thirty-six years old and my husband was thirty-eight. Moreover, I was a psychologist who had worked with families with children with special needs for fifteen years before I had such a child myself. And yet, still we suffered. We couldn't find our balance—everything revolved around what Aviva needed. We knew our marriage and family would be damaged if we didn't protect them from all these stresses.

While Aviva was still in the NICU, Lewis and I met several times with a marriage therapist we had worked with in the past. We found a local support group for parents with children with special needs and started attending meetings. (After six months, we started holding our own support group meetings in the NICU where Aviva was born, knowing we would have liked such a group.) We started working with an early intervention agency just three days after Aviva came home from the hospital, so we had outside support quickly. And most importantly, we read everything we could about having a preemie—and then about how having a child with SPD could affect our family. (We would have loved a book like this one, focused on the special issues of families living with SPD.) We made sure we had some time for ourselves, both individually and together. Friends helped us, staying with Aviva a couple of hours each week so we could have time for each other. What we did was find a way to regain our balance—a way to keep our marriage strong while still doing everything we could to help Aviva.

One of the most important issues in finding your balance is to be aware that it's out of whack. You can't change something if you don't know it needs fixing! It's all too easy to get caught up in your child's issues—they always seem so very urgent. But this is one of those classic situations where you have to take care of yourself first so that you can effectively take care of your child. Think of the standard airline safety guideline: put on your own oxygen mask before putting one on your child, so that you don't pass out and become incapable of taking care of anything at all.

Unfortunately, people often tend to resist change, or deny it's necessary. The bigger the initial change, the bigger the shock (and the emotional reaction), and the bigger the changes needed to regain your balance. When the change is having a child with special needs, the potential harm to the marriage and the family is huge.

Some excellent research recently conducted on fragile families illustrates this point. For the purpose of the research, a *fragile family* was defined as a young couple in poor economic circumstances who had a child without being married, while also experiencing other stresses in their family. When such families had a child with special needs who was identified as such at birth or soon afterwards (e.g., a child with Down syndrome or cerebral palsy), couples were much more likely to break up before the baby was even a year old. This is one of the few well-run studies that supports what families with children with special needs know from experience: marriages and relationships are sometimes damaged beyond repair when a child is identified as having special needs.

RISK FACTORS

There are several risk factors that make relationships more fragile when a child with special needs is part of the family, including differences of opinion, style, and perception; your family's view of the disability; your family's personal history; and feelings of separation and loss. We'll talk about each of these in detail and then explore ways to keep relationships strong and healthy.

Differences of Opinion, Style, and Perception

It's commonly accepted in our society that men and women differ in how they see the world, how they interpret what they see, and how they respond to these interpretations. This is particularly evident when it comes to our children and relationships.

When you talk to families, you hear the same things over and over. One parent—often but not always the mother—gets involved in taking the child with special needs to all the appointments, doctors, school meetings, and therapies. The other parent—again, often but not always the father—goes to work. And works and works and works. Typically, they don't talk to each other about these choices they've made; the more directly involved parent may even feel that the other parent doesn't care enough about the child.

What's going on here is that the couple is responding to the needs of the child in different ways. One parent might feel less able to cope with the direct needs of the child, and feel they can contribute best by making sure money is available for the family's needs. The other may feel guilty or responsible for the child's problems and get overinvolved in a search for a cure or a fix so the family can become normal again—or just committed to helping the child achieve all she can achieve, and as a result arranges a schedule that would be exhausting for anyone. Ideally, of course, both parents find that magical balance between family life, marriage, and care for all of their children.

Research on how the different genders respond to stress and how they express intimacy and love is pretty clear: Women typically want to talk about their feelings; they feel closer to their partners when they feel listened to and understood. Men typically prefer sharing activities with their partners, whether the activity is sex, a bike ride, or just watching TV. (Of course, although these patterns tend to be typical, there are men and women who respond in the opposite manners.)

Personal Reflection

Think about what your personal style is. How do you express your feelings and concerns? How do you think you can best help your family, regardless of what gender you are?

When you have to raise a child with special needs, these differences can be obstacles. For example, one parent might believe that the doctor or specialist of the moment will know best what to do and is willing to leave it all in their hands, while the other parent insists on doing extensive research on all possible options before making a decision. The most important thing to know here is that both ways can be successful and appropriate—these differences only become a problem if the couple cannot agree on how to manage the situation.

Often, it's not just a question of how to arrange doctors, therapies, and schools, it's a difference in the perception of the child himself. Sensory processing disorder is hard to categorize. It's all too easy for a parent or family member to insist that these behaviors must be under the child's control—and that the child is just too lazy, or unmotivated, or rebellious, to get her act together. When parents hold these opposing views, finding a middle ground may require getting outside help. A friend, clergy member, or counselor can help couples find compromises.

Having a child with special needs can cause overwhelming grief and threaten your sense of yourself as an effective parent; it may be hard to accept that your child won't grow up as other children do. It's perfectly fine to take some time to adjust to the changes in your life that will be part of parenting this child. Once again, it's not a problem if the couple sees things differently, it's only a problem if the differences cause conflict or upset.

For me and my husband, the hardest part continues to be that Aviva—now ten—will need lifelong help to be organized. She may never be able to complete all the steps to getting ready in the morning, or to putting together a report, or to cleaning her room, without reminders. I'm constantly telling her teachers this. Once they explain how to do an assignment, they expect kids to remember the task. Aviva doesn't. Lewis and I have to remind both ourselves and others who work with Aviva that she needs help. This constant reminding about her differences is wearing. My husband also keeps forgetting that she needs help, so I'm the reminder-in-charge. Sometimes this angers me, and I want him to pick up his share. Other times, the way things are doesn't bother me, and I'm at peace.

Your Family's View of the Disability

How your child handles his special needs—and even how much he understands about those needs—can be stressful on your marital relationship. Parents often agonize over whether to tell their child the label for their disability or not, and if they do, they worry about how it might impact the child. Personally, I have always talked to Aviva about her issues, and told her the names for those issues. She always knew she was different from other kids; it seemed to help her to understand that her brain was different, too. She knew she would need some kind of help to be successful—now she takes pride in having overcome some of the obstacles she faced. However, this choice isn't for every family. Parents need to decide together if their child is able to understand what is going on and whether or not to tell them about it.

It's important both that parents and child have a common language to talk about the issues they face, and that they work together as a team to help their family run smoothly. If the child accepts the need for therapies, medication, special education, doctor's appointments, etc., the parents will certainly have an easier time of it. If the child doesn't accept the need for these things—or is unable to understand this need because of age or other issues—conflict can easily arise between parents who have different ideas on how to approach the situation. Unfortunately, this relationship conflict will only make the task of adjusting to differences that much harder for the child.

Family History

Another significant factor that can make relationships more fragile is how your family has handled problems in the past. When a family has a history of not being able to resolve conflicts—and perhaps, too, a history of parents and grandparents who haven't been able to resolve conflicts successfully, leaving them with no role models in this area—problem solving will be difficult. Reseach is very clear: marital problem solving has to be learned; it's not a skill we're born with.

Personal Reflection

Consider your own family history. (Think about your family of origin as well as your current marriage and family and any serious relationships you may have been in previously.)

Have problems been resolved successfully in most instances? Or do the emotional conflicts drag on and cause more distress and hurt?

Has your family faced other serious issues, such as loss of a job, death in the family, serious illness, or divorce? How did these circumstances affect your relationship? Did the two of you support each other, offering emotional support and taking care of each other? Or did the situation become yet another source of conflict, leading to fights and arguments? The diagnosis of a child with special needs can be another of those issues that leads to relationship conflict, as parents use blame and guilt and anger to fight their fears for their child and their sadness over the diagnosis.

If you've had both successful resolutions and bad outcomes, can you identify anything you did differently in the successful cases? How can you repeat those helpful behaviors or choices?

Separation and Loss

Families often struggle to accept the diagnosis of their child with special needs. Suddenly the whole world looks different. The life you were dreaming about—the special times you would share with your child, the books you would read, the places you would go, the report cards, the art projects, the hugs and cuddles and smiles—suddenly they all seem distant, maybe impossible. The sadness and grief you feel as a result can both overwhelm you and surprise you—after all, your child is alive; all she may need is some therapy to catch up. Many of us also feel guilty, especially if we ignored or denied the differences in our child; thus we're left wondering whether if we had done something sooner, our child would have made better progress, or at least not been so affected. And when we see a friend's child of the same age, a child who is able to handle change better, or eat more kinds of foods, or is being more successful at school, many of us are reminded of what might have been.

There's a story about having a child with special needs, called "Welcome to Holland" by Emily Perl Kingsley, that has consoled many of us since it was written in 1987. This lovely story describes how a family plans a trip to Italy—reading guidebooks and scheduling all of their outings—and then gets off the plane in Holland, an equally lovely but very different place. This story can help us see that having a child with special needs doesn't have to be a disaster, but instead may just be a different journey, one that may be as beautiful and exciting as the one we had planned.

Beautiful as it is, for some of us, this story just doesn't quite cover the enormity of learning that our child has a disability. Having a child with special needs is much more than simply a different journey—it can be a journey full of pain, conflict, lack of understanding, and hurt. After her child was diagnosed with autism, a mother named Laura Kreuger Crawford wrote the following story.

Holland Schmolland

If you have a special needs child, which I do, and if you troll the Internet for information, which I have done, you will come across a certain inspirational analogy. It goes like this:

Imagine that you are planning a trip to Italy. You read all the latest travel books, you consult with friends about what to pack, and you develop an elaborate itinerary for your glorious trip. The day arrives.

You board the plane and settle in with your in-flight magazine, dreaming of trattorias, gondola rides, and gelato. However when the plane lands, you discover, much to your surprise, you are not in Italy—you are in Holland. You are greatly dismayed at this abrupt and unexpected change in plans.

You rant and rave to the travel agency, but it does no good. You are stuck. After a while, you tire of fighting and begin to look at what Holland has to offer. You notice the beautiful tulips, the kindly people in the wooden shoes, the french fries with mayonnaise, and you think, "This isn't exactly what I had planned, but it's not so bad. It's just different."

Having a child with special needs is supposed to be like this: not any worse than having a typical child, just different.

When I read this my son was almost three, completely nonverbal and was hitting me over a hundred times a day. While I appreciated the intention of the story, I couldn't help but think, "Are they kidding? We're not in some peaceful country dotted with windmills. We are in a country under siege—dodging bombs, boarding overloaded helicopters, bribing officials—all the while thinking, "What happened to our beautiful life?"

That was five years ago.

My son is now eight and though we have come to accept that he will always have autism, we no longer feel like citizens of a battle-torn nation. With the help of countless dedicated therapists and teachers, biological interventions, and an enormously supportive family, my son has become a fun-loving, affectionate boy with many endearing qualities and skills. In the process we've created . . . well . . . our own country, with its own unique traditions and customs.

It's not a war zone, but it's still not Holland. Let's call it Schmolland. In Schmolland, it's perfectly customary to lick walls, rub cold pieces of metal across your mouth, and line up all your toys end-to-end. You can show affection by giving a "pointy chin." A "pointy chin" is when you act like you are going to hug someone and just when you are really close, you jam your chin into the other person's shoulder. For the person giving the "pointy chin" this feels really good, for the receiver, not so much—but you get used to it.

For citizens of Schmolland, it is quite normal to repeat lines from videos to express emotion. If you are sad, you can look downcast and say, "Oh, Pongo." When mad or anxious, you might shout, "Snow can't stop me!" or "Duchess, kittens, come on!" Sometimes, "And now our feature presentation" says it all.

In Schmolland, there's not a lot to do, so our citizens find amusement wherever they can. Bouncing on the couch for hours, methodically pulling feathers out of down pillows, and laughing hysterically in bed at 4:00 A.M. are all traditional Schmutch pastimes.

The hard part of living in our country is dealing with people from other countries. We try to assimilate ourselves and mimic their customs, but we aren't always successful. It's perfectly understandable that an eight-year-old from Schmolland would steal a train from a toddler at the Thomas the Tank Engine Train Table at Barnes and Noble. But this is clearly not understandable or acceptable in other countries, and so we must drag our eight-year-old out of the store kicking and screaming, all the customers looking on with stark, pitying stares. But we ignore these looks and focus on the exit sign because we are a proud people.

Where we live it is not surprising when an eight-year-old boy reaches for the fleshy part of a woman's upper torso and says, "Do we touch boodoo?" We simply say, "No, we do not touch boodoo," and go on about our business. It's a bit more startling in other countries, however, and can cause all sorts of cross-cultural misunderstandings.

And, though most foreigners can get a drop of water on their pants and still carry on, this is intolerable to certain citizens in Schmolland, who insist that the pants must come off no matter where they are and regardless of whether another pair of pants is present.

Other families who have special needs children are familiar and comforting to us, yet are still separate entities. Together we make up a federation of countries, kind of like Scandinavia. Like a person from Denmark talking to a person from Norway (or in our case, someone from Schmenmark talking to someone from Schmorway), we share enough similarities in our language and customs to understand each other, but conversations inevitably highlight the diversity of our traditions. "My child eats paper. Yesterday he ate a whole video box." "My daughter only eats four foods, all of them white." "We finally had to lock up the VCR because my child was obsessed with the rewind button." "My son wants to blow on everyone."

There is one thing we all agree on. We are a growing population. Ten years ago, 1 in 10,000 children had autism. Today the rate is approximately 1 in 250. Something is dreadfully wrong. Though the causes of the increase are still being hotly debated, a number of parents and professionals believe genetic predisposition has collided with too many environmental insults—toxins, chemicals, antibiotics, vaccines—to create immunological chaos in the nervous system of developing children. One medical journalist speculated these children are the proverbial "canary in the coal mine," here to alert us to the growing dangers in our environment.

While this is certainly not a view shared by all in the autism community, it feels true to me.

I hope that researchers discover the magic bullet we all so desperately crave. And I will never stop investigating new treatments and therapies that might help my son. But more and more my priorities are shifting from what "could be" to "what is." I look around this country my family has created, with all its unique customs, and it feels like home. For us, any time spent "nation building" is time well spent.

The birth of a premature baby like mine more often takes one to Schmolland rather than Holland. A neonatal intensive care unit is not a friendly place to visit. But despite the initially severe jolt to our expectations and hopes, Lewis and I learned to look forward to the successes Aviva could achieve. I'll never forget when we received the results of her three-year-old evaluation. We learned that our three-year-old was functioning like a four-year-old when it came to thinking and communicating, but more like a two-year-old when it came to physical tasks like running and jumping and writing. Lewis looked at me and said, with tears in his eyes, "Her brain works."

Feelings of loss and grief are major contributors to relationship distress and divorce. When couples can't move past their pain, the stress on their relationship can become enormous.

SEVEN CHALLENGES TO A HAPPY MARRIAGE

Over many years, the coauthors of my previous books and my partners in the Prevention and Relationship Enhancement Program (PREP) have conducted extensive research into divorce prevention/marriage enhancement, tracking and studying couples over long periods of time. My colleagues have identified seven challenges to maintaining a rich marriage. (My thanks go to Howard Markman and Scott Stanley for our long and fruitful partnership working on PREP and David and Claudia Arp for sharing their work on this with me.)

Challenge One: The Challenge of Forgiveness

Let go of past marital disappointments, forgive each other, and commit to making the rest of your marriage the best.

Forgiving your partner for past hurts and disappointments is a difficult process. The research on successful marriages is clear, however: without forgiveness, relationships get stuck and can't move forward. Whatever has happened in the past, if you want your family to succeed, you need to move on and learn to work together.

Many marriages and partnerships have been destroyed by accumulated damage from resentment and a lack of forgiveness. This damage sets up a barrier to intimacy. Forgiveness is not only a great expression of love and commitment, it's critical for maintaining your intimate bond.

What is forgiveness? People offer many different answers to this question. My colleagues and I in marriage education view forgiveness as canceling a debt. When you forgive something, you're committing to no longer holding this offense against the other person. You're releasing the other person from the one-down position the person has ended up in because of whatever it is the person did. The you-owe-me idea, whether voiced aloud or not, will no longer be part of the picture. In essence, forgiveness is giving up your perceived right to get even.

Forgiving is a conscious act of the will—a choice. Forgiveness depends on your choice to let go of the past, regardless of what your partner chooses to do.

Personal Reflection

Have you ever purposely said something hurtful to remind your partner of a past offense? Maybe in the middle of a fight? If so, looking back, how do you feel about having brought it up? We pay a price in pain and hurt in our relationships when we hold on to past offenses.

What Forgiveness Doesn't Mean

Forgiveness isn't forgetting. Most of us can remember the most painful things done to us by others if we think about it. In fact, most of us don't ever forget such things, unless we suffer brain damage. Though "forgiveness is forgetting" is a common saying, it actually sets up an expectation that most people cannot meet—we simply don't forget the things that hurt us. However, that doesn't mean we can't forgive them.

Forgiveness isn't accompanied by an absence of pain. One can forgive and still be grieving for a loss. Grieving and feeling pain doesn't mean you haven't forgiven. The damage might be ongoing—or just take time to repair.

Forgiveness also doesn't relieve your partner of the responsibility of doing the right thing—by forgiving, you've simply committed to not holding the other in debt, you haven't affected the other's behavior or choices at all. Ideally, the one giving offense takes full responsibility for their actions and offers a commitment to change. Sometimes, in more extreme cases, a person may forgive another but choose not to reconcile with that person until destructive behavior patterns have been changed.

Steps to Forgiveness

Sometimes, you need something more. Forgiveness is often a process that takes time. You may need to work through a specific event or issue together to get to forgiveness. The following set of structured steps offers a road map to forgiveness.

1. Set an agenda to work on the issue in question. Schedule a time without kids, TV, interruptions, or other plans. Plan to talk about one issue at a time. Both of you must agree that you're ready to discuss it.

2. Fully explore the pain and concerns related to this issue for both of you. This may take more than one talk, and may take a much longer time than you expected or hoped. Be patient. You may need to learn better communication skills to do this successfully. (You'll find some ideas for impoving your communications skills in challenge three: effective communication.) Most important, please talk to each other with respect and genuine caring.

3. The offender asks for forgiveness. Apologies are powerful but not enough—you must ask for forgiveness. Look for ways to validate the feelings and hurt of the one offended.

4. The offended agrees to forgive. This means you agree to commit the issue to the past, with no attempts to get even, and no holding your partner in debt. This means you don't throw the issue at the other in a fight at some later date. It's over.

5. If applicable, the offender gives a positive commitment to change recurring patterns or attitudes that give offense. This can range from remembering to do household chores without being asked, to giving up alcohol, to not having another affair. If the offensive patterns don't change, the offended partner has a tough decision to make about the future of the relationship.

6. Move forward; work together to protect and strengthen your partnership.

Challenge Two: Creating a Partner-Focused Marriage

Create a relationship that is partner-focused as well as child-focused.

This is a particularly important challenge for a couple who has a child with special needs. Couples need to remember the reasons they became partners in the first place. The dynamics of any relationship change after having children; they change again after the identification of a child with special needs. Roles and functions that previously worked may no longer be relevant. It's important to refocus and redefine your relationship to bring it back to a state of balance.

Another piece of this challenge is commitment or dedication. Couples who are dedicated describe themselves as a team, willing to do things that will help or support their partner. They plan for their future as a couple and think about how to reach goals as a couple, not just as individuals. They look for what's good for their marriage, not just for what's good for themselves as individuals.

Personal Reflection

Identify some of the roller-coaster highs and lows in your marriage.

To what, or whom, in the relationship do you attribute the relationship's ability to weather crises?

How have your roles changed since you had children? Or how do you think your roles will change now?

What can you do as a couple to develop "we-ness?" To focus on each other?

What is one thing—concrete, practical, and achievable—that you will do, individually or as a couple, to meet this challenge?

Challenge Three: Communicating Effectively

Maintain an effective communication system that allows you to express your deepest feelings, joys, and concerns.

Practicing good, clear communication is probably the most important thing you can do for your relationship and your family. We all know how easy it is to fall back into bad habits when in the midst of an argument. These negative patterns can be very hurtful. However, there's a tool you can use together to stop ugly arguments right away, even before you learn any other skills. If even just this one tool becomes part of your regular communication practice, you'll find working together much easier.

It's called the *time-out*. And it's exactly what you think it is. A communication time-out gives you a way to stop something negative that's happening and turn it in a new, safer direction.

Taking a Time-Out

Decide with your partner in advance—*before* you need to take one—what words you'll use to call for a time-out. You can use anything that signals that "we need to take a break now." My male colleagues usually choose to say "time-out" itself, but I prefer a simple "stop." Or you could choose something unusual. For example, one couple I know uses the word "hamburger" when they realize they've gotten into an escalating argument. The word not only stops them from hurting each other, it usually gets them laughing, which really cools things down.

Either you or your partner can call a time-out at any time, and both you and your partner agree to respect the other's need for a time-out. Calling a time-out isn't the same as withdrawing from a conversation or refusing to talk. It's a respectful way to reduce the emotional temperature of a heated argument, a way to give people the chance to pull themselves together before facing a tough talk.

After a time-out is called, decide together whether to drop the issue for the time being but come back to it later, or shift into a safer way of talking by using the speaker-listener technique, which is described a little later in this chapter.

You can start using the time-out right now, whenever you need it. Even after you learn the speaker-listener technique and other safe ways to handle conflict, you can still call for time-outs. Just remember: issues don't go away if you never discuss them. If you choose to postpone dealing with important problems, be absolutely sure you *do* deal with them later.

Pausing: Taking a Mini-Time-Out

If a discussion starts to escalate—or you see it's just not going well—you can take a time-out and come back to it at another time. Or you can simply pause the conversation for a few minutes.

As with a time-out, either you or your partner can call for a pause at any time. Both of you agree ahead of time to stop talking as soon as someone says "pause." Then, you either both take a break for a few minutes before trying again, or you restart the conversation in a calmer, more respectful way. To keep from returning to a negative cycle after a pause, you might want to say something like, "Let's forget what we both just said and start over." The key is to keep moving forward and not get stuck in the past.

Some general guidelines can help keep communication safe and helpful. Even if you choose not to use some of the specific skills we'll discuss later in the chapter, these guidelines can still make a difference:

- Make sure you have your partner's complete attention before you say anything important—and that you're giving your full attention to him or her. Make it easier to listen to each other by first eliminating distractions; find a quiet place to talk and agree not to answer the phone or doorbell.

- Don't assume your spouse is ready to talk just because you are. Ask first if it's a good time. If the answer is no, agree on a time you'll both be willing and able to have a good conversation.

- If you come home in a bad mood because you didn't make the sale you thought was a sure thing, tell your spouse not only what happened but that it's put you in a bad mood. Knowing what's happening will help your partner react more gently to something angry or defensive you might say. But remember: being in a bad mood doesn't give you the right to treat your partner with disrespect.

- Try hard not to be a mind reader; don't negatively interpret what your partner says because you think you know what was *really* meant. Don't assume the worst.

- Think about how your style differs from your partner's. Talk about how these differences affect your relationship. Being aware of your differences can help you be more respectful of each other and prevent misunderstandings.

- Always try to discuss things gently and with humility; this will create an atmosphere of trust that will lessen fears of rejection and increase openness and understanding.

Personal Reflection

What are three things you can do before beginning a conversation with your partner to make it more likely that you can really relax and hear what your partner says? Think of simple things, like turning off the TV or taking a bubble bath. Think about how doing these things first could have helped you during previous talks.

Consider how you usually start discussing issues with your partner. Are you distracted or involved in another activity? Are you afraid of what might happen? Do you assume the worst? Are you calm, attentive, and positive?

Think about your style. Are you generally outgoing and straightforward? Do you tend to hold back until you're more comfortable? What's your spouse's style? If you have very different styles can you think of a way to bridge these differences so you can talk more easily together?

Think of a time when you and your partner recalled an event in completely different ways—and ended up arguing about it. What can you do to keep that from happening again? What are some of the techniques you've used in the past to keep your conversations pleasant, productive, and respectful?

Creating a Safe and Supportive Environment

There are two main times when couples have trouble communicating well: when they disagree about something like money, parenting, or who's supposed to do what around the house; and when they talk about sensitive issues like sex or loneliness. These conversations often don't go well because one or both of the partners is afraid that talking will frustrate them or that they'll be rejected because of something they say. Typically neither partner feels safe. As a result, they end up either having a frustrating talk or fighting. Or they don't talk at all.

Communicating without fear is absolutely essential to a great marriage. The deepest kind of intimacy only develops when partners feel safe enough to say anything and everything to each other. (Research also shows that feeling safe at home—and protected from destructive parental conflict—is very important to the well-being of children.)

What's needed is an agreed-upon, step-by-step structure for your important conversations. Structure can keep discussions and emotions from racing out of control. Structure can prevent frustration and chaos. Structure is a powerful tool that assists clear, open, safe communication. In our books about couple communication, my coauthors and I explain a highly successful, structured communication method we call the *speaker-listener technique*.

Using the speaker-listener technique: The speaker-listener technique is a simple, effective approach to communication that can help you and your partner develop confidence that you can handle whatever problem comes your way as a team, and without fear—and that will do much to put you on the path to a long and loving marriage!

If the two of you already talk openly and safely, even when you disagree or feel vulnerable, you may not need to learn this technique. If you choose not to, be sure you both agree that you already talk well about important issues.

Guidelines for the speaker-listener technique:
Rules for the speaker:

- Speak only for yourself. Express only your thoughts, feelings, and concerns—not what you think are the listener's concerns.

- Use "I messages" to express yourself. For example, say, "I got angry when you forgot to call me," not "You didn't care about me enough to call." (Be careful: although sentences like "I think you don't care about me" may sound like "I messages" they're not. Although these sentences may start with "I," they actually express opinions about the listener, *not* what the speaker feels.)

- Don't talk on and on. Say what you need to say in small, manageable chunks. That way the listener can take it all in. You'll have plenty of chances to say everything you want to say.

- Stop after each statement so the listener can sum up and repeat back to you what you just said. If the listener's paraphrasing isn't quite right, gently make your statement again in a way that helps your partner understand. Stop and restate your words until the listener gets your point completely and says it back to you.

Rules for the listener:

- Paraphrase what the speaker said each time the speaker stops. This means briefly repeating what you heard, in either the speaker's words or your own. If you didn't understand something that was said, ask the speaker to explain further. Then paraphrase these words. Keep doing this until the speaker lets you know you've paraphrased the words correctly.

- Don't argue with what the speaker says or give your opinion about it, just listen carefully and paraphrase what the speaker tells you. Wait until it's your turn to be the speaker before making any response of your own. When it is your turn, respond respectfully and gently.

Rules for both the speaker and the listener:

- When the speaker is talking, the listener cannot talk or interrupt. To remind both of you that the speaker has the floor, the speaker can hold something that represents that concept, perhaps a piece of carpet or linoleum, or whatever's handy. You can always just write "I have the floor" on a piece of paper or cardboard and have the speaker hold that.

■ The speaker and the listener should take turns speaking and listening. The speaker goes first, with the listener listening. Then the two switch roles (passing the piece of carpet or flooring if used), and the listener becomes the speaker. Keep switching roles so that each partner has as many opportunities as needed to both speak and understand. If the speaker asks a question, the listener should paraphrase that question to make sure it was understood before the speaker passes the turn to the listener, so the listener can become the speaker and answer the question.

■ Both speaker and listener can call for a pause at any time. A pause can be especially helpful if the listener starts giving opinions or the speaker says too much for the listener to paraphrase. Pausing also lets you get out of a negative pattern and clear the air.

■ Focus on having a good, safe discussion, not on solving a particular problem. If you're thinking about a solution, you're less likely to really hear what your partner feels about the issue.

As you use this technique, it's important that you both listen carefully and show respect for each other—even if you strongly disagree with what your partner said. This means not making faces, not rolling your eyes, not shaking your head, and not muttering under your breath. It also means waiting politely until it's your turn to speak. (Remember: you're a team, you want this process to help.) When you have a safe way to communicate, sensitive and emotional issues can be discussed without fear.

Challenge Four: Using Anger and Conflict Creatively

Use anger and conflict creatively to build your relationship.

The following approach to resolving problems is based on four important points:

1. All couples have problems. It's not the presence or absence of problems that predicts whether a marriage will last, it's the

way couples handle the angry, upsetting emotions that go along with the problems that really matters.

2. Couples who are most effective at solving problems work on them as a team. They don't fight against each other, but instead work together against the problem.

3. Most couples hurry to solve their problems. This may not give them the necessary time to address all the concerns involved, especially hidden ones. If unaddressed, these concerns can resurface. Quick fixes don't last.

4. Not every problem can or needs to be solved.

Sometimes simply accepting differences is what's necessary. This is another situation where men and women often think about things differently. Typically women are the ones who bring up current problems—but that doesn't mean their goal is always to solve them. Most wives say they simply want their husbands to listen to them, not necessarily fix their problems. Women value airing problems and talking about issues openly.

However, men typically prefer to do something more active than just talk. Men tend to want to solve problems, fast and simple; as a result they often feel helpless—and may even withdraw—when they think they can't. Instead of plunging in to try to fix things, both men and women need to listen to each other's issues first, calmly and constructively. The way you begin communicating about a problem is crucial to eventually solving it together—or just deciding to accept and value the differences between you. In fact, many couples tell us that the need to solve a problem can disappear entirely after a good talk.

Many people don't want to believe that there are problems that can't be solved. Even just the idea of such problems can affect a couple's feelings about their marriage: if their problems can't be solved, there must be something wrong with their marriage. Thinking this way isn't constructive—fearing something is seriously wrong can make you think the two of you should divorce. To protect your happiness, you want to do the best you can to solve your problems, but it's important to understand that you may not be able to solve every problem that comes your way; even the happiest of couples have issues they've lived with for the whole length of their marriage.

Having a child with special needs isn't something that can be solved. Rather, couples need to learn how to handle any resulting conflict or stress by communicating clearly and openly about their concerns, as discussed in challenge three.

Steps for Handling Problems

1. Discuss the problem; if you have good communication skills, use them here. If you need some help with this, use the speaker-listener technique outlined in challenge three.

2. Solve the problem:

    a. Set an agenda: focus on one topic at a time, without distractions.

    b. Brainstorm: work together to think of as many solutions as possible. If conflict comes up while you're brainstorming, go back to step 1 (discussion) until you both feel heard and understood.

    c. Agree on a solution: decide on something to try, not necessarily forever, just to see if you can work things out. Agree to give this solution a fair chance without hesitation or reluctance.

3. Follow up: make a plan to talk again in a couple of weeks, to see if the solution you agreed on is working. If not, use your best communication skills to talk about the situation and go through the problem-solution process again to decide on a new solution to try.

Challenge Five: Deepening Your Relationship with Your Spouse

Build a deeper friendship and enjoy your spouse.

When you ask people why they married their partner, most people say that their partner was their best friend. Couples don't marry because they need a partner to do laundry with or fight with. They marry because life with a best friend is richer and more satisfying. But when life becomes stressful, time for friendship often gets lost somewhere amidst housework, homework, business obligations, and the normal exhaustion of family life. When you add in therapy, doctor's appointments, and consultations with schools and specialists—as well as the added time needed to parent a child with SPD—friendship starts to feel unattainable. Unfortunately, friendship with your partner can feel like a luxury, not a necessity.

However, the truth is the exact opposite: friendship is a necessity. Friendship is like the oxygen mask on the plane—you need it to breathe deeply so that you have the energy and concentration you need to care for the rest of your family. Friendship renews us, helps us find the strength to go on; friendship shows us we're not alone—we have our beloved partner at our side.

Personal Reflection

Think back to when you and your spouse started dating. Did you go to the movies? Out to eat? Did you go for walks and hold hands? Did you laugh and smile a lot? Did you act silly? Did you talk all night? Did you think there wasn't anything better in the whole world than spending an evening together, just the two of you?

Now think about last month. Did you and your partner share a lot of fun times? How many dates did you have with no one else along? Do you remember laughing together over something really silly? Did you go on a walk, play miniature golf, share burgers and a video, or hang out in a bookstore?

If you can think of several times in the last month when you and your partner played together and really had fun, your team is on a roll. You can use the following activity to help keep it that way. Or, if your friendship with your partner has weakened under the strain of family needs, use this activity to help restore it.

ACTIVITY: MAKE A FUN DECK

Get a pack of index cards. Write—both of you—at least a dozen suggestions for activities you'd like to do, one suggestion per card.

Make some suggestions low cost or no cost—maybe watching the sunset, taking a walk, having a candlelight dinner, taking a shower together. (And don't forget sex!) Also, include some fun going-out activities, like dancing, biking, going to the theater, or trying new restaurants. Whatever you both enjoy—or something new you'd like to try. Go hiking or take a painting class. Be adventurous.

Next, mix up the cards. Choose a night when you can have a date together and make arrangements for the kids (a date is just for the two of you). For each date, one of you chooses three cards from the deck. The other then selects one of those three and makes it happen. Enjoy!

Conflict affects everyone. If you deal with conflict when both of you are ready and able to talk, it won't destroy your fun time. Use your best communication skills to handle issues during time you specifically schedule to talk calmly about these issues. If conflict erupts during times meant for fun, call a time-out and talk about the problem later. Fun times need to be exactly that: fun. Conflict should never be allowed to intrude.

For some couples, just realizing how important it is to have fun will be enough to start having more of it; some couples already build in time for a movie night at home, popcorn and all. But most couples need more than just the occasional time together.

Most couples think it's not all that romantic to schedule time for fun together. But given the realities of daily life, it's often necessary—just go ahead and mark your calendar. Planning ahead ensures that you do other important things; it will do the same for fun. It will also give you something pleasurable to look forward to, which can help reduce stress.

If you need to arrange for a babysitter for an evening out, do it at the same time you schedule your date. Choose someone you know and can count on so you'll be relaxed and unworried when you head out the door. Sometimes, when you have a child with SPD, finding the right person can be the hardest part. Talk to friends, family, and your support group to find someone both you and your child feels safe with. Another family with a child with SPD may be willing to trade baby-sitting time.

One thing to remember: because people are usually so busy, it can take a bit of time to wind down and relax on a date. If you can't relax, don't panic. If you need to talk about the children, do. Just remember not to talk about issues that bring up conflict. Instead, share positive moments. After a little while, the pleasure of being together—and the chance to relax and play—should help you focus on just the two of you being together as friends.

Challenge Six: Renewing Romance

Renew romance and restore a pleasurable sexual relationship.

Well, this one seems pretty obvious! Close physical intimacy is necessary for a healthy and successful partnership. In the early stages of most relationships, sensuality and sexuality are very high priorities. Couples tend to touch a lot and make love often. By being intimate in these ways, they deepen their connection, give and receive pleasure, and learn more about each other. Physical intimacy brings partners closer together and strengthens their love.

Unfortunately, physical intimacy often loses its top spot on our priority list after the first years of marriage. With the responsibilities of work, home, and family crowding around us, less time is often given to showing and sharing physical love.

I'm not going to spend too much time on the sexuality piece of the equation—I'm going to assume you can figure that out, especially since you've had at least one child! (However, if you're having problems with your sexual relationship, check the resources section at the back of the book to find some help.) I do, however, want to remind you that sex isn't all there is in a close intimate relationship. *Sensuality*—the ability to feel things through our senses—plays an important role as well.

Sensuous acts include things like hugging, holding hands, smoothing your partner's hair, kissing your partner's neck, running your hand down your partner's bare arm, massaging each other's feet, snuggling while listening to music, feeding each other popcorn, and intertwining your arms to drink champagne on your anniversary. For some couples it may also include a teasing kind of athletic sensuality, such as massage. Sensuous acts can happen in bed, in the kitchen, at the beach, or just about anywhere. Sharing sensuous time together can help you and your partner reengage with each other, and remind each other of the strength there is in your team.

Challenge Seven: Replenishing Your Spirit

Evaluate where you are on your spiritual pilgrimage.

Research on religion and marriage is very clear: couples who share religious and spiritual beliefs and practices do better than couples who have differing beliefs and practices. It's not the specifics of the differing religious beliefs or practices that can constitute a problem, it's the conflict between the partners over how to express such beliefs and practices. Having a child with special needs can put extra stress on a couple already dealing with conflict around faith issues; divorce and breakup rates are higher for interfaith couples.

Some couples choose not to include a spiritual component in their lives; this is a valid choice. You may find the social and emotional support you need in other ways—perhaps through your friends and family. For those who *have* chosen to include spiritual components in their lives, the social and emotional support offered by a congregational setting of any kind can be extremely powerful. When parents disagree over where to seek such support, it can cause tension and conflict. Excellent resources exist to help interfaith couples deal with such conflict. Speak with your clergy to locate such help; use the communication and problem-solving skills we've explored in this chapter to talk about these issues and find a solution that works for both of you.

FINAL THOUGHTS

I want to wrap up this chapter by reminding you of what you read at the beginning: life is all about balance. When you think about the needs of your family, you also need to think about the needs of your relationship with your spouse. Your marriage can be the cornerstone of your family, can give you strength and help you manage all the needs of your life, your children, and their special needs. The correct life balance for you may not look like anybody else's. It doesn't matter: there's no one right way to balance your life—there's just your way.

Chapter 4

Dads Are Needed, Too!

For decades the role of mothers in child-rearing has been the focus of popular media and the research community. As a result, it's clear that mothers play an important role in the growth and development of their children. Certain aspects of motherhood appear to be universal. A study commissioned by the Mothers' Council (Erickson and Aird 2005) found that mothers have many experiences in common, regardless of their backgrounds, their geographical locations, and their life circumstances. For example, all of the mothers in the study derived great satisfaction from being moms, were concerned about the negative forces impacting their children, and wished for a culture that would make mothering less challenging.

I have to echo the report's finding about the great importance of a mother in a child's life: mothers are very important. It's only been over the last decade or so that there's also been a growing interest in the role that fathers play in the lives of their children, revealing their importance, too. Consider the following points:

- Children who feel close to their fathers are significantly more likely to enter college and significantly less likely to have a child in their teen years, be incarcerated, or show various signs of depression.

■ Young males are significantly more likely to engage in criminal activity when raised without a father (and even more likely to do so if they live in a neighborhood with a high concentration of fatherless families).

■ Father involvement is considered a significant factor in developing *empathy* (the ability to understand how others feel).

■ Children of involved fathers are more likely to receive appropriate health care and less likely to be injured.

■ Father involvement is equally important for the behavioral outcomes of boys and girls (National Fatherhood Initiative 2000, 2002).

If one or both of your parents didn't do a great job, your own parenting skills don't have to suffer. Some men deprived of good fathers in their own lives are able to respond by being very involved dads themselves.

Some people suggest that although many fathers truly want to be involved, divorce makes it difficult, if not impossible, for many dads to be actively involved in their children's lives. However, the Fragile Families study of a *birth cohort* (a group of people all born around the same time) of nearly 5,000 children found that

many fathers who live separately from their young children and children's mothers are highly involved with their children, thereby dispelling the notion that living separately from children is an insurmountable obstacle to fathers caring and providing for their children. (Center for Research on Child Wellbeing 2004)

Being divorced doesn't have to mean being uninvolved. Caring for your children needs to happen no matter what your marital status, where you live, or how you feel about their mother.

DIFFERENT STYLES

Fathers and mothers tend to support their children in very different—but equally valuable—ways. Not understanding these differences can lead a parent to put down the other's input—or characterize the other's style of participation as wrong or uncaring or caring too much. If one parent intimidates the other enough to withdraw, the biggest damage suffered is to the child: as a result this child won't get to experience the best of having both parents involved in her life.

One of the best things my wife has ever done for me is leave me alone with our three children, dog, and cat for a weekend. I confess, even though I'm an involved parent, I was nervous at the thought of shouldering all of this responsibility myself. We had a lot of fun during that weekend, however—we played outside all day, went out for ice cream, and got really dirty.

It was empowering for me to know that I could still be a successful parent without the support of my wife. Fathers need these opportunities to sink or swim. A father weekend will in all likelihood be quite different from a mother weekend. I can tell you that my children's clothes won't match and we'll barbecue all the time; I'll also let my children sit in my lap and drive the car into the garage.

While it can be difficult to give up control and let things be done differently, it can also bring you a sense of freedom. Knowing that our children can be well cared for by either of us has given me and my wife both the confidence to parent alone if the need arises and the ability to let go of some control and allow the other to step in.

DIFFERENT EMOTIONAL RESPONSES

Stereotypically fathers—and men in general—tend to be characterized as unemotional or angry. While this may be true of some fathers, it's certainly not true of all. The fact is, mothers and fathers respond to distress in very different ways. Fathers are typically more task-oriented while mothers are typically more relationship-oriented. Fathers tend to process emotions internally, while mothers tend to process emotions by expressing them directly.

For example, if my wife is distressed, she'll immediately seek someone to talk to about how she's feeling. If I'm distressed, I need time to understand how I'm feeling; I might take a walk or hit golf balls. Once I know how I feel, I then begin to think about how I'm going to solve the problem. If we were to come together while we were both distressed, I might only want to talk about what to do, while my wife might only want me to listen. The key to dealing with distress in a healthy manner is in understanding how moms and fathers respond differently to distress and respecting this diversity.

A Conversation with J. Neil Tift

To understand more clearly how fathers respond to having a child with SPD, and learn new ways to support fathers, I spoke with J. Neil Tift. Neil is the director of professional advancement for the National Practitioners Network for Fathers and Families (NPNFF). NPNFF is a nonprofit membership organization with about 780 members around the country—including both men and women—that advocates on behalf of organizations serving fathers through technical assistance, consultation, and training. Neil has been with NPNFF for the past five years. Neil has also been a father for twenty-nine years; two of his children have special needs.

A Father's Point of View

Moms and dads respond to distress differently. A lot of times moms react to a diagnosis of SPD with what we call *expressive crisis*. Often mom's response is on a more gut and emotional basis. Mom is more focused on what emotional impact this disability will have—how will this affect my child's siblings, the extended family, our relationship—as a mom, as a dad, and as a couple?

A lot of times, I see dads respond to the diagnosis with what we call an *instrumental crisis*. Dads look at how is this going to impact the family long term—what's it going to cost, am I going to need more medical insurance, am I going to need to beef up my medical insurance because these prescriptions are going to cost more? Dads tend to look more at the concrete details and fulfilling their role as provider. For example, if the dad sees that they're going to need more money because this is going to cost a lot more, some fathers go out and get a second job. This isn't bad—I mean, he's not doing anything wrong—but he's abandoning the mother at the exact time she really needs him to be home more, both to deal with this child with SPD and to just deal with the emotional complexities. So, it's not that fathers don't look at the emotional component; it's that fathers focus on the health insurance, the cost, etc.

Moms—again generalizing to some extent—tend to be concerned about the child's ability to be happy. The dad, a lot of times, is concerned with this question, "Will my child be able to do the things other children do?" Another response dads often experience is grief over the loss of the ideal child; what we need to do with those fathers is help them accept the child for who he or she is. Sometimes for the mom, her concern is about time for herself. A typical response to this is to overcompensate, to spend a lot of extra time with the child. Moms burn out in ways that are physical and emotional. Fathers tend to burn out more just from taking that extra job, or worrying about the financial stuff.

A lot of times too, dads are left out of the process. When my daughter Hanna was six weeks old, I took her to her well-baby appointment by myself—my wife had something else going on. I brought Hanna in and I sat in the largest teaching hospital in Minnesota—a very good, very high quality hospital. I sat there for over an hour; finally I went up and said, "What's going on?"

They said, "Oh, we're waiting for her mother to come." I had to explain that her mother wasn't coming, but that I was there and I was ready to deal with the well-baby checkup.

A couple of weeks before that, when we went in to talk to her dietitian, the nurse kept looking at my wife and not looking at me. Finally, after about ten minutes, I put my face right in front of my wife and said, "You know, I'm here too."

The nurse said, "Well, you know the mother is the one who brings the baby into the world."

I replied, "Hanna's adopted."

Fathers of children with SPD encounter another layer of challenges where a lot of times, the system already doesn't expect them to be there. I think the way that we address these challenges is by offering support for fathers of children with SPD and chances for dads and children with SPD to do things together—but not exclusive of mom; you need to have families together.

One of the biggest things that would help fathers is to understand their own emotional status—be able to put their fingers on the pulse of how they are doing. One of the most helpful ways to accomplish this is the support group for fathers, but I also have found that calling it a support group can be the kiss of death. What was most successful was to have some activities where it was dads alone and others where it was dads and children.

[Neil also suggested seeking opportunities to have mothers talk to other moms, and fathers to other dads. After that, couples may find it easier to talk to each other about how they are feeling.]

Part of the diversity of mothers and fathers is that when a baby is one month of age, moms will hold the child the same way ten times out of ten. Fathers, on the other hand, will hold the child differently nine times out of ten. The lesson to learn from this example is that what is important is that the child is held, not *how* the child is held.

—J. Neil Tift
    Director of Professional Advancement,
    National Practitioners Network for Fathers and Families
    Father of two children with special needs

HOW MOMS CAN HELP DADS BECOME MORE INVOLVED

If you're reading this book, you're probably a mom, not a dad. And, too, you're probably looking for a recipe to get dads more involved. Before we get to that, let's talk about some of the challenges dads face.

Recognizing Things Aren't the Same for Moms and Dads

As Neil describes, most social service organizations are predominantly female. For example, out of a staff of sixteen, I'm the only male employed in the Denver Mayor's Office for Education and Children. Just as it can be uncomfortable for women to visit highly male-dominated businesses, it can be uncomfortable for men to attend back-to-school conferences in female-dominated preschools or elementary schools.

Work

Despite the many changes in our society over the past few decades, men still tend to be the primary breadwinners of the family. Many men work much more than forty hours a week. Don't make assumptions that the father of your child works so much because he wants to escape the family—consider that maybe he's working so hard in order to provide for his child in the best way he knows how.

Boys and Feelings

Also, peers and parents still often pressure boys to be unemotional. I know that I tried very hard not to cry when hurt, teased, or disappointed. As an adolescent and young adult, I found that I was very good at being unemotional. Just because the father of your child doesn't express his feelings doesn't mean he doesn't have them. It may mean he's uncomfortable expressing them and needs your support to do so.

The Recipe for Engaging Fathers

Children need to have their fathers involved in their lives. Whether a mother is reading this or a father is, the same actions can help make that happen. If you're a mom, invite your partner to read this chapter, too. If you're a dad, try any of the following activities you're not already doing. Your child will thank you for it. The recipe for father involvement includes:

- Having both fathers and mothers attend appointments

- Fathers seeing the strengths of their children

- Fathers finding opportunities to talk to other fathers of children with SPD, in person or online

- Everyone—fathers and mothers and professionals working with their children—understanding that fathers may be supportive in ways different from mothers

I also suggest allowing fathers to parent in their own ways. For example, if your husband has dressed your daughter in mismatched clothes, let it be—try to just appreciate the differences of his parenting style. Susan tells the story of eight weeks she spent in the hospital while pregnant with her second child. Every afternoon her husband brought Aviva, then almost four, to see her mom, so they could have dinner together. The first day, Susan was very upset when she saw Aviva's uncombed hair and mismatched clothes. But by the next day, Susan had realized that those aspects were extremely unimportant compared to the fact that her husband was successfully caring for their daughter alone. Aviva was fine; she was enjoying both her full-time day care and having special time with her dad. This realization made their future visits much less stressful. In fact, even after she returned home with their second baby, Susan was much more able to just let things slide. The moral of the story is: unless a particular approach is truly unsafe, allow a father to parent in his own style.

Another Family's Perspective

Doug Gertner is a father who is highly involved in his family. Two years ago, his son Jordy was diagnosed with SPD. Psychological tests found that Jordy's verbal skills were significantly higher than his performance or motor abilities. As a result, physical tasks such as writing, playing soccer, or catching a ball are much more difficult for Jordy than for his peers.

Doug exemplifies many of the key points of father involvement. First, it's clear that being involved is a high priority for Doug. Second, he's free to be open as a father; he has found his style as a father and this is acceptable to his partner. Third, Doug focuses on the strengths of his child—he looks for what Jordy can do. And finally, Doug has created some family traditions that he carries out regularly, even when it may seem that his child doesn't appreciate them. I bet that later on, Jordy will remember those notes in his lunches very fondly indeed.

Jordy's Story

At an early age, Jordy craved rough and tumble activities. It's not in my nature to be physical, but I indulged him because I saw how much joy it brought him. At the park, though, he was always cautious about play structures. I thought he was wise. In pre-school, he was behind the curve. I always tried to look at his strengths—I wasn't disappointed that he wasn't going to be the world's best athlete.

The greatest challenge was getting him to try new things—it's still a struggle to this day to get him to try new foods, to try to find food on vacation, anything new. We've bent over backwards to get him what he wants. I know what four things he is going to want for lunch—a peanut butter and honey sandwich, closed and (only recently) with crust, Pringles, apple slices (again only recently) with the peel, and one of two flavors of yogurt.

I've never packed a lunch without a note. Usually the note is about something we're going to do. I try to look at the positive. Because I know exactly what he wants for lunch and it's easy, I have time to write him a note. I don't know if he reads them anymore, but it's a tradition.

When the diagnosis was made, I swallowed hard and did as I was told. The hardest part was taking him to the hospital for occupational therapy (OT) because of the stigma. I didn't miss any of the sessions, though. My partner and I always went together. I was there when he and his therapist were making obstacle courses, and when she was trying to get him to eat other foods.

At first the therapy seemed like voodoo. Within just a few sessions we became devotees because it started working. His pet blanket disappeared; he went across monkey bars; he became much more adventurous. When he started OT, Jordy had a fear of going through tunnels. Thirty sessions later, he was designing obstacle courses and putting in tunnels.

I've gained patience, which is the cornerstone of father-hood anyway. I've learned to accept where Jordy is and not expect him to be somewhere he's not. I try to celebrate the things he's good at. I've learned how to help him with things he still needs to work on. Some things he's good at, some things he's not.

I've been blessed with a partner who understands, is open, and is able to articulate SPD as who Jordy is and describe it in simple, understandable terms. She makes it so neither of us freaks out or is ashamed by the fact that Jordy has needs.

It's been a gift to see Jordy and his therapist work together and see benefits and changes. Jordy plays soccer now. I've watched him become able to get in there and play with a zeal and aggressiveness that he would not have had if he had not had occupational therapy. I enjoy seeing him getting in there and having fun and making a contribution to the team.

In spite of how open we've been about the process, I would still like a stamp that says "cured" on his forehead. I'd like a sense of closure. His therapist agreed to run Jordy through the Sensory Integration and Praxis Test (SIPT) again as a post-test. We're expecting the results soon. I know that issues are still there, but unless there is a strong recommendation otherwise, we want to pull Jordy out of occupational therapy. We're kind of ready to say he's done well, he's doing fine, let's give it a rest for a while.

—Doug Gertner, Ph.D.
Fatherhood advocate

Personal Reflection

If you're a mom, think about how you help your children be involved with their father. If you're a dad, think about the opportunities you take to be involved with your children. (Remember: there's no right or wrong way to do this; don't feel shame or assign blame. You may not want to share your answers—that's perfectly fine.)

A child benefits most when mothers support fathers and fathers support mothers. Consider the following questions:

For mothers:

What do you most appreciate about your child's father?

What are some of his strengths as a parent?

If you could change one thing about him what would it be?

Do you find yourself correcting him? How often? Under what circumstances? How does he respond to your corrections? Is there a better way to do this? (Think carefully about how you insist things be done. Limit your corrections to things that really matter.)

As a child, what did you see as the role and responsibilities of the father?

As a child, what did you see as the role and responsibilities of the mother?

What are your greatest gifts as a mother?

How can your child's father support you so that you can be an even better mother? How can you communicate this?

For fathers:

What do you most appreciate about your child's mother?

What are some of her strengths as a parent?

As a child, what did you see as the role and responsibilities of the mother?

As a child, what did you see as the role and responsibilities of the father?

What are your greatest gifts as a father?

How much time do you spend with your child on a daily basis, on average? Is that enough? Would you like to spend more time? How can you make that happen?

Do you have a network of fathers you can talk to?

Do you attend parent-teacher conferences and doctor's appointments?

How can your child's mother support you so that you can become an even better father? How can you communicate this?

GETTING FATHERS INVOLVED

Fathers need to see what their children can do. When fathers understand the strengths and challenges of their child with SPD, they're less likely to overprotect or set unrealistic expectations. Knowing their child's strengths can also alleviate some of the emotional strain caused by the worry that peers may not accept the child.

The remainder of this chapter is aimed at providing fathers with activities to support their child with SPD. This is intended to help fathers put together activities on their own that are both fun and tackle an area of SPD appropriate for their child. Fathers should keep in mind as they create activities that the *child* drives the activity; the father is merely the guide.

Activities for Fathers and Kids with SPD

Most men find it easiest to have a relationship with their child by doing activities together. If you read to or have long talks with your child already, congratulations! Please do more of that, too.

The first step in developing activities to support your child is to observe her for a while, perhaps over several different days. What does she like to do? Left alone with unstructured time, what types of activities does she pursue? What does she avoid? Does she prefer activities inside or outside? How does she arrange her room? Does she like music? If so, what kind? Consider asking such questions of her teacher or coach. Try to find out as much as possible about her.

Use this information to plan activities. It's not your job to be a therapist, so don't feel any pressure to act like one. Your job is to help your child by playing with her. So, if she likes crashing into things or hitting people, arrange a time once in a while when she can do these things in a safe, controlled way. You might plan a time to wrestle, or have a pillow fight. You might play soccer outside. Tie activities into her strengths, interests, and motivations.

For the Child with Sensory Modulation Disorder

This is the child who varies in response to sensory information. If your child frequently spins, crashes, or jumps into your arms, try to think of games or activities that can channel this energy. It might help to think of activities that *you* do when you are stressed—maybe heavy work like gardening or carrying groceries, or things like playing basketball, soccer, swimming, or running.

If your child avoids certain things, try to think of games that could gradually increase your child's tolerance to these things.

ACTIVITY: FEEDING THE SENSORY MONSTER

What do you do in response to different feelings, such as being stressed, angry, excited, bored, etc.? How do you get yourself to focus? What do you find soothing?

To have your child begin to identify *his* sensory needs, he needs to both think creatively and understand cause and effect. Brendan loves to play a great cause-and-effect game we call the What-If Game. First, I pose a question such as, "What if we could touch the clouds?" Brendan might respond, "Then we'd be giants!" Then it's Brendan's turn to pose a question. As you continue to play the game, start to pose questions about feelings. If your child asks you a feeling question, such as, "What if you were angry?" your response should be an honest statement about your sensory needs if you felt angry. For example, you might respond, "Then I would pound on some clay."

Eventually, begin talking about activities your child can do in response to different feelings. We call this Feeding the Sensory Monster—you're teaching your child to pound pillows instead of his brother, splash water in the sink instead of in bed, take deep breaths instead of whine or moan. If you or your child likes to draw or collage, you can make a poster with faces expressing feelings on one side, and pictures of activities on the other. Or, if your child is older and reads well, write out feelings and activities in different colors. Use whatever works for your child.

Practice this by looking mad, or sad, or confused and having your child figure out what activity to do to help handle the emotion you're displaying, then do the activity together. Whenever your child has one of these out of control feelings, remind him to check his list or poster.

ACTIVITY: MAKING A MOVIE

Children of all ages like to be seen on television. If you're feeling especially creative, your child might enjoy spending a day making a movie. This is a great activity that can be done during any season.

The first step is to develop a basic story. What is the setting? Who are the characters? What is the problem and climactic event? What is the conclusion? Once you have agreed on a basic plot, let your child take the lead in gathering props and costumes—it's required that your child be allowed to be costume and makeup designer! Your role, once your child is excited and involved, is to be a support. Allow her to be the leader.

The end product isn't so important. In fact, you may never even get to filming it. What is important is the time spent together. Also, by taking a supporting role and allowing your child to lead, she will naturally engage in activities that satisfy her sensory needs. Again, your role is that of a facilitator: help her find the resources she needs and guide her to activities that are appropriate, but let her lead.

For the Child with Sensory Discrimination Disorder

For this child, the primary goal of activities is to help him become better able to use his senses to interpret his surroundings. You want your child to become more in tune with his senses. A nature walk is always fun. Or you could cut a hole in a shoebox, place different objects in it, and see if your child can reach in without looking and identify each object. Or you could play in a sandbox, digging tunnels and searching for treasure. The following activity is the indoor version of this:

ACTIVITY: TREASURE HUNT

First, make pirate hats. Everyone in your family, young and old, needs to get into the spirit of the game. Pirate hats can be made simply by stapling two sides of two large triangle cutouts together and then placing it over the head—or you can find more detailed directions for making a paper hat in *Curious George* by H. A. Rey (a great book to read with young children).

When everyone has made and decorated a hat to their satisfaction, go into the kitchen and get a large bowl. Next, get out either a five-pound bag of flour, several packages of dried beans, or some rice. Have one of your children dump one of the above items into the bowl. The captain then has everyone scatter and secretly gathers some items—spare change, plastic letters, small pieces of candy, or any other small items—be creative. Mix the secret items into the beans, rice, or flour so they can't be seen. Now call in your eager pirates, and take turns reaching into the bowl to find treasure. For increased difficulty, you can do this blindfolded.

For the Child with Sensory-Based Motor Disorder

Obstacle courses are a fun way to build coordination. Just make sure that although the obstacle course is challenging, it's not so difficult that it becomes frustrating to your child. Remember: your child drives the activity; you are merely the guide. Have your child create the course, and have your child help you think of games to play.

ACTIVITY: MUMMIES, MUMMIES EVERYWHERE!

For this activity, you'll need a bulk quantity of toilet paper. I suggest you buy one of the really big packages, with twenty-four rolls.

When you're ready to begin, gather everyone together. Have your children stand in the middle of the room, hands at their sides and feet together. Now, wrap lots and lots of toilet paper around each of them. (If it's healing to think of this activity as parental revenge, allow yourself the freedom of the thought.)

When your children are all bundled nicely, set up an obstacle course—this might involve jumping over pillows, hopping to the left or right, or turning in a circle. Structure the course to be fun for your children, taking into account what kind of skills they already have—and that they're wrapped in toilet paper! Make sure the course has both a beginning and an ending point.

Have your children complete the course; when they get to the finish line, let them break out of their wrapping.

With this activity you both provide sensory input to your child with SPD, and give her an opportunity to develop her motor planning skills. Best of all, your child probably didn't even notice—it was too much fun!

FINAL THOUGHTS

It's important to have fathers positively involved in the life of a child with SPD—and it doesn't have to be hard. You don't need to be an occupational therapist to be purposeful in the activities you do with your child. The activities presented are just the beginning. Get to know the strengths and challenges of your child so that you can develop your own games. Games don't have to be formal with rules and turn taking. A game can be as simple as just having fun playing with your child. As you develop your own list of activities, I encourage you to log on to our Web site (listed in the resources section at the back of the book) and send us an e-mail. We'll post your activities there for all to share and enjoy.

Chapter 5

Taking Care of Siblings

As I've mentioned in previous chapters, my oldest brother Roger displays autistic behaviors. On the autistic spectrum, Roger is high functioning and has several savant characteristics. For one thing, he's a walking almanac. One evening, I challenged him with the toughest question I could think of: I asked him how many countries were created as a result of the breakup of the Soviet Union. Not only did he immediately tell me the number (fifteen), he also listed them in alphabetical order.

In the mid-1960s, a psychiatrist recommended that Roger be placed in the state mental institution. At the age of five, he was still nonverbal and at times could be violent. My parents didn't agree. Instead, they provided him with extensive early intervention supports paid for out of their own pocket. He was placed in a private preschool that specialized in children with special needs. He was given Thorazine, a powerful antipsychotic, to help manage his behavior. And every Saturday for seven years, father took him to see a psychiatric social worker. The support we received from this social worker made the difference; not only did the social worker see Roger at his office, occasionally he also came to our house to help my parents understand how to manage my brother's behavior at home.

Roger entered first grade two years behind his peers and had special education support until third grade. He graduated from high school without special education support, went on to Indiana University, and graduated with a bachelor of science degree after ten years of sheer persistence.

My other brother, Tom, and I had our share of difficulties. Tom is still resentful about how he was treated by Roger and the relative lack of attention he received from my parents, much more so than I. Tom remembers being assaulted by Roger and having his personal space invaded. On one occasion, when Tom was working on a model airplane in the garage, enjoying the peace and quiet of being alone, he suddenly had an uneasy feeling of being watched. He turned around to find Roger glaring at him. Not only was Tom frightened, he felt as though his privacy had been permanently trespassed.

I had the benefit of being eight years younger than Roger. This helped put some distance between us, but being his brother was still difficult. Roger has always been a broken record; he asks the same questions over and over again. It was embarrassing as a child—and sometimes still is—to be with him in public. On one occasion, he was even questioned and patted down by a police officer who thought he was on drugs because he was talking to himself and displaying odd mannerisms.

I often wished that Roger had an obvious physical disability so that people would know that he had special needs. His hidden disability was even more hidden because for most of his school career, he was in regular education classes. Except for our closest family friends, very few people understood his disability.

Growing up, I was labeled the normal one. I was the only one who had regular friends. I was the only one who had an interest in dating. Both Tom and I had significant, although different, pressure placed upon us. Tom is brilliant and was always expected to be a scholar. I was expected to have a family and friends and keep the harmony. Being labeled—even as the normal one—made me feel alone, isolated.

What I mourned most was the absence of a role model. I felt that as the youngest, I was supposed to have an older brother who could talk to me about dating and show me how to play sports. I was supposed to have an older brother blazing the trail. I felt like I was going through childhood alone, without a mentor.

To add to the complexity of our family dynamics, Roger was—and still is—extremely resentful of anyone suggesting that he has a disability. About a year ago, when I gathered up the courage to ask him if he thought he had special needs, I thought he was going to kill me, right there in the restaurant. I will never forget his look. At the time, he was forty-two years old.

I understand Roger's desire to feel normal and fit in with the rest of society—he just wants to be like everyone else. For me, however, it seems as though everyone in the world should recognize that he's different. I want to talk about it, I want us to acknowledge that there's a disability in our family. I feel as though there's a gag stuffed in my mouth. I can't help thinking that if Roger would just acknowledge that he's different, we could become closer.

Growing up, Tom and I felt isolated. We couldn't talk to our peers about our feelings because there was a lack of understanding and information within our own family. When people teased and tormented my brother, I didn't know what to say; I didn't know what to do with the anger I felt. When my mother passed away in 1988, in addition to my grief at her passing, I felt the added stress of wondering about our family's future. How would our family's estate eventually be divided? Who would assume responsibility for Roger's long-term care? What would happen when my father passed on?

Until the early 1990s, information and resources to support siblings of children with special needs were sparse, when available at all. Siblings were a largely forgotten group. Tom and I were forgotten siblings. I don't want your children to be similarly forgotten.

SIBLING SUPPORT

Frequently, siblings of children with special needs have different responsibilities and face different expectations than their peers. This is most true for older sisters. Often, older sisters are expected to assume a maternal role, a role possibly lasting a lifetime. While there is scant research on siblings, some researchers have questioned whether these additional responsibilities are harmful to the emotional well-being of brothers and sisters.

Studies show that siblings of children with special needs are at greater risk for anxiety, depression, poor self-concept, and cognitive problems (Kupper 1993). It's easy to understand the reasons behind these increased risks. You know the challenges of raising a child with SPD—imagine parenting without adequate information about SPD and an understanding group of peers. This can easily lead to a feeling of helplessness. Siblings of children with special needs are often expected to assume significant responsibility for them, but without the proper tools and without a support group. When raised in an environment devoid of information, but with increased responsibilities and increased expectations, brothers and sisters can end up mourning a lost childhood.

A Conversation with Don Meyer

Don Meyer is the director of the Sibling Support Project of the Arc of the United States. The senior author and editor of five books, Don has conducted workshops throughout the United States, England, Italy, New Zealand, and Japan to raise awareness of the needs of siblings. In the following interview, Don describes the concerns and hopes of siblings of children with special needs and details some of the best ways to support the siblings within your family.

The Sibling Experience: Unique Concerns, Unique Opportunities

My work with brothers and sisters originated out of work with fathers of children with special needs. In 1978, while a graduate student in early childhood special education, I had an advisor who was unhappy that fathers weren't coming to her so-called parent programs; she asked me to do something about "these fathers." I welcomed the opportunity to help start the University of Washington's Fathers Program and ran it for its first eight years. I'm glad to say the Fathers Program (now called the Fathers Network) is still going on in the Seattle area. It wasn't long before we started to see other traditionally underserved family members who were affected by the presence of the child's disability and created SEFAM— Supporting Extended Family Members—at the University of Washington's Experimental Education Unit.

On any given Saturday, I might be running a Father's Program meeting, a Sibshop (a fun, interactive, and supportive workshop for siblings), or a Grandparent's Workshop meeting. I still do workshops on and about grandparents and dads from time to time, but since 1990 my work has been almost exclusively with brothers and sisters of folks with special health and developmental needs.

Siblings' experiences parallel parents' experiences. Our basic argument is that brothers and sisters have many if not most of the same issues that parents do—as well as some that are uniquely theirs. Secondly, siblings are going to experience concerns longer than anyone. They may be in the lives of their brother or sister longer than any service provider will, most likely longer than the parents. We're talking about a relationship that could easily exceed sixty-five years. This makes a powerful argument for why we should be thinking of brothers and sisters at every turn. Yet, still I frequently have to remind our colleagues—even those who worship at the altar of family-centered services—that brothers and sisters are part of the family.

One workshop that I frequently conduct is called Brothers and Sisters: Unique Concerns, Unique Opportunities. It's my belief that, throughout their lives, brothers and sisters will experience an array of unique concerns that other people their age simply won't experience. However, mixed in with those unique concerns are some unique opportunities for growth. To acknowledge these opportunities is not to be Pollyannaish about it or view the experience through rose-colored glasses. Quite honestly, a lot of that growth sibs experience is hard-won growth, but it's growth nonetheless.

Among the concerns we discuss during workshops is *over-identification*. In other words, some kids may wonder whether they might have whatever it is their brother or sister has. If a sib has a brother with a severe learning disability, and he's having a hard time regurgitating whatever facts he needs to regurgitate for an exam, he might find himself thinking, "Gee, I guess Mike's not the only one in the family with a learning disability." Other concerns some sibs experience include isolation and a lifelong, ever-changing need for information. Specifically, brothers and sisters have concerns about what's going to happen to their sib with special needs in the days to come—and what their roles will be in that future.

There are lots of different kinds of guilt that brothers and sisters can feel—whether it's feeling like they were spared the disability, or feeling bad that they were angry with their brother or sister with special needs. They might feel guilty that they can do things their brother or sister can't do.

Siblings might feel resentment when the world seems to revolve around their brother or sister, or resent the different expectations placed upon them. For some, there are increased caregiver demands. And others may feel a pressure to achieve—to be the "good kid" in order to balance the scales.

But opportunities are important to acknowledge, too. Many siblings are characterized by maturity and a responsible attitude that goes beyond their age. This may be because they've had to handle responsibilities that other kids their age haven't even considered—there aren't too many thirteen-year-old girls who, when watching their eight-year-old brother, have to deal with poopy pants. But if your little brother's still marching up the learning curve when it comes to toilet training, that might happen on your watch.

Siblings might be more mature because they've developed some patience from interacting with their brother or sister. They might be more mature because they've developed diplomacy in answering questions posed by total strangers. And they've certainly had to make sacrifices on their sibling's behalf.

Another unique opportunity these siblings can have is insight into the human condition. I don't think anyone can have a family with a disability and not have an expanded view of the human condition. One of the real joys of doing Sibshops is hearing these frequently profound thoughts come out of the mouths of little kids.

Tolerance is another unique opportunity. Many brothers and sisters realize that there are many different ways to be in this world. It's okay to be different. These sibs are the ones who reach out to that kid who is perceived as being different—the kid who comes to school midyear, doesn't speak English, weighs more, or is a different color. They'll step up for other kids who have special needs—kids who aren't even their sibs.

Typically-developing sibs are often inspired by their brothers and sisters who have disabilities. They may comment that "my brother working at Target is like me being the senator from the state of Colorado. If he can do this, there's no end to what I can do." There's an appreciation for other things that people take for granted, like the blessing of good health. There seem to be vocational perks, too. Many siblings like you, Chris, end up in helping professions. They are proud of their siblings' abilities and tend to look at their siblings in terms of what they can do, not what they can't do. Many of them are fierce advocates for people who are perceived as different, and at a time when peer pressure means a lot.

One of the things we're beginning to see is people like you and other adult sibs going into what most of us would consider true leadership positions in various organizations. There's a lot to be hopeful for.

On the needs of siblings of children with hidden disabilities:

Every disability has its own challenges; hidden disabilities certainly do. For instance, at the Sibshops I might see one sib of a child with autism say to another sib of a child with Down syndrome, "Well, when your brother acts up in public, people know there's a reason." People will excuse the behavior of someone who looks a little different more than someone who looks like everyone else.

Then there's the identification/overidentification issue that's more likely to happen in the mild or invisible disability. It's also more likely to happen if the child with special needs is older than the typically-developing child. I myself grew up with an older brother and sister who both have seizure disorders. I grew up thinking it was only a matter of time before I started having a disability myself—that was sort of the family tradition into which I was born. Back in the '50s no one talked about having a seizure disorder because it was associated with mental illness.

On the whole, however, there are more similarities than there are differences between having a sibling with an apparent physical disability and having a sibling with a hidden disability. When your brother embarrasses you in public by passing gas at the restaurant, singing during the church sermon, or melting down at the supermarket, the fact that he has Down syndrome versus autism is probably only an academic difference for the brother or sister who's royally embarrassed.

On Sibshops:

Sibshops are meant to provide the same kind of common-sense peer support that parents get out of a good parent-to-parent program. They are provided to the family member who will have the longest-lasting relationship with the individual who has the disability.

When we look at the services and consideration that brothers and sisters get vis-à-vis the services and consideration parents get, it's easy to see who's getting the short end of the stick. The scarcity of opportunities to connect with one's peers is real evidence of that. One of the things that my project does is host several listservs having to do with sibling issues. One of them—SibNet—is for adult sibs. Every week it seems we get a posting from a sister—because it's usually the sister who picks up the care of the sib—who writes and says she feels like she's been reading a diary as she viewed postings from other sibs. She might be forty-something years old. Forty years is a long time to wait for valida-tion. We would never make parents wait forty years to meet their peers. If just about anyone were to have a newly diagnosed kid, the first thing we would do is introduce that parent to another parent. This doesn't happen to brothers and sisters. That's what we're trying to do with Sibshops. We want to con-nect peers and information, but to do it in a recreational context.

We want something that really emphasizes wellness, where they talk about common joys and common concerns with other kids who get it. We want these to be rewarding on many levels. We don't want to be the programmatic equivalent of spinach—or perceived as one more way that my sister's screwing up my life. We are unapologetically playful.

At Sibshops, kids spend a lot of time playing new games, doing craft and cooking activities. Tucked in here and there for good measure are opportunities to talk about the good parts and the not-so-good parts of having a brother or sister with special needs. Participants might learn how other sibs handle difficult situations, like what to do when someone calls your sister a retard. They might talk about what to do when you want your parents' attention but they're consumed with your brother or sister with special needs. They might learn more about their brother or sister's disability. I try to make it a format that I would have liked when I was ten or eleven.

On the importance of communication:

Communication is key in every family, but in families where there is a child with special needs, it's mission critical. I think parents should do whatever they can to foster the best possible communication they can have with their typically-developing kids. Doing so will alleviate a lot of the concerns brothers and sisters might have if they're worried about the future, having troubling feelings, or having difficulty with peers.

If these sibs can talk to a parent or some other trusted adult, that's going to help immeasurably. When I do workshops with parents, I encourage them to avail themselves of courses in active listening, which are a part of parent-to-parent trainings. The same principles used to communicate with adults can also be used with one's children.

I also recommend *How to Talk So Kids Will Listen and Listen So Kids Will Talk* by Adele Faber and Elaine Mazlish. It's an incredibly parent-friendly book. I also encourage parents to carve out time out of their crazy, busy schedule to spend time one-on-one with their typically-developing kids. It might be a trip to Burger King or a walk around the lake—just something to let them know by deeds and by words that they're important. Sometimes it requires some creativity. I've had some parents tell me that every month or every other month, they pull their child out of school and spend the day together. They play hooky together. They might go for a drive, go out to lunch, go shopping, or get their nails done, but whatever they do, they talk and they talk and they talk. Whatever schooling the child may have missed that day is more than compensated by the relationship maintenance they've had. Parents need to work toward getting the kind of respite they need to spend time with their typically-developing kids and have a little break themselves.

I know a sibling whose parents didn't attend her high school graduation when she was the valedictorian because they didn't believe they could leave her brother with anyone else. I've met sisters who have reported that their wedding day was dictated by the needs of their sibs with severe disabilities.

Advice for parents:
I have seven suggestions for parents:

1. Provide siblings with age-appropriate information from a variety of sources. Service providers, if they are really interested in families, have an obligation to make themselves available to siblings. We need more voices and information for this group.

2. Provide siblings with opportunities to meet other brothers and sisters. Obviously I'm invested in Sibshops, but that's not the only way. They can meet through our listserv called SibKids, or in the pages of books, such as my *Views from Our Shoes* or *The Sibling Slam Book,* which are aimed at teen sibs. Families can also just arrange to meet sibs from other families.

3. Parents should work toward having the best possible communication they can have with their typically-developing children.

4. Parents need to set aside time to spend with their typically-developing children.

5. Parents should learn more about life as a sibling. There are some really good books about this, including *The Ride Together* by Judy Karasik and Paul Karasik, *Riding the Bus with My Sister* by Rachel Simon, and *Special Siblings* by Mary McHugh.

6. Parents need to reassure their typically-developing children by making plans for the future of their child with special needs—and they need to share these plans with their typically-developing children. I've seen too many instances where parents have not been planful for the future and it's caused a lot of anxiety for the typically-developing child.

7. The single strongest factor influencing a child's interpretation of a sibling's disability is their parents' interpretation of the disability. Consequently, if the parents perceive it as a life-searing tragedy from which there's no escape, they shouldn't be surprised if their kids perceive it that way, too. However, if they perceive it as being a series of challenges to meet with as much grace and humor as they can muster, then they have every reason to believe that at the end of the day, their typically-developing children will perceive it that way as well.

—Don Meyer
    Director of the Sibling Support Project,
    Arc of the United States

Communication and Information

As Don mentions, effective communication is critical to the support of every member of your family. Effective communication means that members of the family actively listen to one another and manage everyday conflict capably. This might include listening to each other's feelings about a particular problem, identifying acceptable alternatives, establishing consensus, and having follow-up to determine if the problem has been sufficiently addressed. There are lots of resources available to help with communication issues (see chapter 3 as well as the resources section at the back of the book for some suggestions).

It's important to understand that your children may grow up to dislike each other as adults. This is natural and happens to many sibs, whether or not one of them has special needs. Children grow up to be adults with distinct personalities; sometimes these personalities don't mesh well with those of their siblings. If this proves to be the case, it's doubly important that your children have a healthy relationship with you—both you and your children will be better off emotionally as a result. The best way to accomplish this is to share information and model effective communication.

Developmentally Appropriate Communication

Siblings need to have developmentally appropriate information not only to relate more fully to their sister or brother with special needs, but also to be able to talk with their peers. It's not enough to tell your typically-developing children that their brother has sensory processing disorder. Even most adults don't understand what that means.

I've found that a good approach is to provide both an example of something that the child with SPD does well and an example of a challenge. The fewer words you can use and the more concrete you can be, the better. You want to be able to give your typically-developing child a quick statement to use when peers ask—as they inevitably will—"What's wrong with your brother?" A quick statement can be all that's needed.

First, think about how you would characterize your child's most significant strength. Some words that might come to mind might be: smart, creative, endearing, charismatic, funny, or thoughtful. Next, how can you sum up your child's most significant challenge in a single word? (This word needs to be acceptable to your child with SPD.) Some words that might come to mind could be: distractible, forceful, loud, or sensitive. (Be careful about using sensitive to describe a boy. Unfortunately, depending upon the age of the child, it can lead to peer ridicule.) It might help to create a two column list as in the example below:

Strengths	Challenges
Smart	Distractible
Curious	Loud

Can you use these descriptions to make a quick, two-adjective statement that provides just enough information to satisfy curiosity? For example, "My child is _____ ." The purpose of this statement isn't to be technically correct or all encompassing. This statement is intended to be a tool your children can use to handle the difficult situation of having to explain their sib to others. For example, Brendan's description of himself is "smart and hyper." To be fair, consider coming up with a statement for each of your children. Do it for yourself, too, and then share it with your children—they need to know that everyone has both strengths and areas of challenge.

Personal Reflection

How do you feel about the relationship between your children?

What do your children see as each other's strengths and weaknesses? How do you know this?

What are you doing to support each of your children, including the typically-developing children?

Do your children feel supported by you? Is the support that you're providing actually beneficial in the eyes of your children?

What steps can you take to better support each of your children, so that all of your children grow up feeling appreciated and valued?

A Conversation with a Sibling of a Child with SPD

To help understand the needs of young siblings of children with SPD, I interviewed twelve-year-old Nicole. (I must say, however, that Nicole is twelve going on eighteen; she's very mature for her age.) Nicole has a seven-year-old brother whose mother and he nearly died at his birth. As an infant, he was diagnosed with failure to thrive. He received early intervention supports, but at the age of seven still has significant sensory needs. In school, he receives information-and-language-processing support as well as motor support.

A Sibling's Point of View

CA: *What are you most concerned about with your brother?*

N: He gets frustrated a lot. I might say something that he might not get and he'll get frustrated and go to his room. I feel like I've done something wrong. I feel disappointed. I don't know if I've done something to offend him or not. I usually don't mean anything bad, but he might not get it.

CA: *Do you think he has special needs?*

N: Sometimes, not usually. He's just like a normal kid. When he was little, he didn't eat anything though. The only way that I can tell that he has special needs is that he gets frustrated really, really easily.

CA: *Does he have tantrums?*

N: Yes.

CA: *What do you do then?*

N: I try to calm him down. I try to sit him down and try to talk to him because sometimes he won't listen to my parents. Because I'm closer to his age, I can relate to him better.

       He gets frustrated easily and has friends who don't take him seriously—they don't always get it because they don't know that he has special needs. His friends might also have an easier time reading because reading is one thing that we really need to work with him on. He does have difficulty with that. But he's made so much progress that you can't really tell he's disabled.

CA: *What's the best thing that parents can do for siblings?*

N: Be very patient with them. Help them understand what's wrong with their sibling. Sometimes I don't get in my head that he doesn't interpret everything that I say. What I need to work on is that I think of him as a normal kid, and when I'm bothering him and that confuses him with his special need, I don't get it. I don't realize sometimes.

CA: *Would it help if parents talked to you and explained what was going on with your brother—how he learns best?*

N: I think the best thing for other siblings to know is that they might not always get it they have a sibling with special needs. I think parents should talk to them about what's wrong and ways to be with their sibling—like being more gentle.

CA: *What is the best thing about having a brother with special needs?*

N: I've learned that all people are unique ... I feel kind of special that I have a brother with a disability because I've learned so much more than if I didn't have a brother with special needs. I've learned that respecting people is very important.

CA: *Do you think that you're more patient than your friends?*

N: Yes, when I have friends over and he asks if he can play too, they might say no. I usually say yes. If I didn't think it would be fun for him, I would try to find something fun for him to do. Nothing against my friends, but I think they should be a little more patient with him.

CA: *Do you feel embarrassed when your friends come over, or when you're out in a restaurant with him?*

N: Sometimes. Sometimes he blurts out weird noises—weird things—that's one of the things he does that I get embarrassed about.

CA: *What do you do?*

N: I try to tell him, "Can you please not do that?"
        He'll do it again.

CA: *Do you get breaks at all? Does it help?*

N: Every day after school he has a tutor who helps
        him read. I'm always alone here at home during
        that time. I get to do my homework and I get to
        think. When he gets home, it changes. If I was
        watching a TV show that he doesn't want to
        watch, we have to find something that we can
        both agree on.

CA: *If you were to give advice to other siblings, what would
        you tell them?*

N: Patience—lots of patience.

CA: *What if they had a hard time with that?*

N: Count to ten in your head. Calm down. Talk to
        your parents.

        —Nicole
          Twelve years old; sister of a boy with SPD

When I interviewed Nicole, I was struck by her sense of responsibility for her brother. For example, when she described her brother's difficulty with reading, she said that "we" needed to work on it. Although this does suggest that unfair responsibility may be being placed on Nicole in her role as an older sibling, I also got the sense that her interest in helping her brother with reading was truly out of love.

I was also surprised to hear that her respite came from being home alone, particularly given the many news reports about latchkey children being at risk. To Nicole, however, this time alone at home provides her with the opportunity to think, focus on homework, and just enjoy the quiet.

One key lesson to learn from both Don and Nicole is that it's important to talk with your children to learn how to best support them.

Although you may feel guilty about leaving your child alone at home, this may be exactly the form of respite he really needs.

WAYS TO SUPPORT SIBLINGS

It's not just parents and the children with disabilities who need support—siblings do, too. Don't let them be forgotten while tending to the needs of everyone else in the family.

Provide Respite

Just as you need time away to be a better parent, children need time away to be better siblings. I was usually able to create my own respite through friends. However, it may take some effort to discover what kind of break will benefit your child, particularly if she's shy. Perhaps she would like some one-on-one time with a parent. Or a special place to draw, read, or just be alone. Respite can also come through extracurricular activities. Your child's school, the YMCA, or the local parks-and-recreation department can be good sources of information. Remember: respite must be in the eye of the child. Don't coerce your child into doing an activity just so he has time away.

Develop a Positive Relationship with Each of Your Children

All parents with more than one child hope that their children grow up to support and love each other. However, it's important to realize that as our children develop their sense of self, they may discover that they don't share many interests with their siblings. They may grow up respecting each other, but not particularly eager to spend a lot of time together.

Your goal is to develop a healthy relationship with each of your children, so that each feels valued and important. It would be a tragedy for any of your children to grow up feeling that their needs were ignored.

Develop Effective Communication

Effective communication is critical for the family of a child with SPD. Assumptions about what others want or need can inhibit the free flow of communication. Ideally, you want to create an open environment so that everyone feels free to express their individual needs. If nothing more, it's important to ask sincerely and listen with an open mind. (For more on creating effective communication, see chapter 3.)

Talk about important issues with your children. If your child with special needs is going through a change in medication, let all of your children know. If you're stressed about work, share that, too—in an age-appropriate way. However, remember: parents are ultimately responsible for issues affecting the family, not children. If you share that you're stressed about work, it's also your responsibility to share what you intend to do about it.

Assume Parental Responsibility

Just like the captain of a ship, as the parent, *you* are ultimately responsible for everything that happens to your children. Older siblings, especially sisters, often assume more than their charge for siblings with special needs. However, children need the opportunity to fully establish their own self-identities; too much responsibility can hinder them from doing so.

Most significantly, it's your responsibility to manage behavior and set expectations. Children should not be expected to shoulder this burden. Among the adult siblings I've spoken with, this is clearly the biggest source of resentment—adult siblings often express frustration that as children they were expected to help manage behaviors that were well beyond the control of their parents.

Provide Fair Rewards and Credit

Of all areas, this is where I struggle most. As you work toward managing the behavior of the child with SPD, so much attention can be focused on her that you lose sight of your other children. Inevitably, you will need to answer, "What is fair?" For example, while your typically-developing child may be rewarded for being regularly on the honor roll, you might similarly reward your child with SPD simply for keeping his hands to himself. The child on the honor roll will eventually ask why the other is so well-rewarded for something that seems so trivial.

Have your children work with you to set goals that are a stretch, but achievable. Teach your children to understand that everyone progresses at their own rate. When measured in this way, your children will come to realize that the effort needed to reach both of these goals may be similar.

Share Information

Unfortunately, very few books mention siblings. When you go to school, the doctor's office, or just about any other service provider, the topic of siblings will arise only very rarely. Thus, it's particularly important that in this climate, you don't overlook the needs of your typically-developing children. As Don described, their experiences parallel yours. They need just as much support as you do, perhaps more. Share information, talk about SPD, and be open with them.

Include Siblings in Family Planning

Siblings need to know what the long-term plans are for the child with SPD. Siblings aren't naive—if there's a question about whether the child with SPD can be totally independent as an adult, they'll wonder if the responsibility of caring for their sibling will fall on them. A lot of anxiety can be relieved simply by putting concrete plans for the care of the child with SPD in place, and then sharing these plans openly when siblings are old enough to understand.

Family planning can also be the focal point for a rich discussion. What are your children's hopes and dreams for the future? What are their plans for being independent? How do they see each other's needs? How do they see reality now and in the future? Remember: you don't know how anyone feels about an issue until it's on the table in open discussion.

Personal Reflection

If you have siblings, what was your relationship with them as a child? As a teenager? As an adult?

How have you nurtured relationships with your own siblings? Why is this important to you?

What have you observed in the relationships between your children? How do they get along and how do they support each other? Is there conflict and tension between them that requires adult intervention?

How have you nurtured relationships with each of your children? Why is this important to you now? In the future?

FINAL THOUGHTS

Healthy relationships—both between siblings themselves and between siblings and parents—are the goal here. If children have bad feelings about how they're treated compared to their sibling with special needs, it will negatively impact your relationship with them as adults.

The most important factor in supporting siblings is being positive and proactive about any disability that impacts your family. This doesn't mean that you have to ignore challenges; instead, model how to address the challenges in healthy, constructive ways.

Remember: just as adults need respite to be effective parents, siblings need respite to be effective siblings. Make sure they have plenty of opportunities to engage in their own interests and have positive social opportunities with their friends.

Lastly, communicate openly with all of your children. When making decisions regarding the child with special needs, include siblings in the discussion—in an age-appropriate way. Also, communicate plans for the future; siblings need the sense of security that comes from concrete knowledge, whatever future plans may be.

Chapter 6

Learning to Talk About SPD

You think you've got things under control: after all, you have a diagnosis for your child that you understand pretty well; you've learned to work with doctors and therapists; you and your partner have talked about protecting your relationship; and you're sensitive to the needs of your other children—and then, suddenly you realize that you have to see your whole extended family at the next holiday dinner and questions will come up about why your child won't eat cranberry sauce, has to have all her foods separate on the plate, and can't play tag with her ten cousins who are running all over the house. Or maybe when you take your child to the community swimming pool, he screams when another child splashes water on him. You get the idea. How do you explain this complicated diagnosis to family, friends, and strangers?

To add spice to the mixture, you may also have to deal with cultural communication issues. You or your partner may feel that talking about your child's disorder would be harmful to her and her self-image, or that such things are private, to be spoken of only within the family. While trying to protect your child from harm is an excellent goal, choosing not to explain her disability can have negative consequences for the child, her siblings, your marital relationship, and your own emotional health. In this chapter, we'll explore some of the challenges people face in talking about their child with special needs, as well as some ways to more successfully do so.

TALKING TO YOUR FAMILY

Many of the skills we've already talked about—specifically in the chapters on relationships, siblings, and fathers—can be applied to communication within the family. To further build on these skills, let's focus now on the five essential elements of effective communication.

The Five Essential Elements of Effective Communication

1. The first element of effective communication is being physically and emotionally available to communicate. It's easier to establish positive relationships between family members if they have multiple opportunities to be together and share.

2. The second element is communicating clearly and directly. Say what you mean and ask for what you need. If you have a disagreement with a family member, talk to that person directly, don't vent to someone else.

3. The third element is listening. Listening is perhaps the hardest part of effective communication, but can also be the most rewarding. To listen you must actively try to understand what the other person is saying, paying attention to both verbal and nonverbal messages. Let the other person know you're listening by briefly paraphrasing what has just been said and asking clarifying questions.

4. The fourth element is being supportive of the person with whom you are communicating, and being aware of this person's level of understanding. If you ask questions of your child, you may need to be very specific in what and how you

ask. Any questions you ask should be supportive, with the purpose of understanding another person's viewpoint more completely.

5.   The final element is being positive. It's boring to hear some-one complain all the time. In a healthy work environment, if you have a complaint, you follow it up with a suggestion for change. Establish the same ground rule at home.

Tips for Good Communication

Raising children can bring out both the best and the worst in us. None of us is perfect. Even though we may try to hide it, we often still have our own baggage to deal with. In many respects children can be a mirror; in them, we see our own strengths and weaknesses, which can be difficult.

Particularly when daily stress builds, children may say or do some-thing that hits a nerve. If you begin to lose control, take a time-out, step back, call someone else to take over, and forgive yourself. Let go of the situation. If you have yelled at your children, apologize—that goes for both mothers and fathers. Use "I messages" to explain how you felt. For example, "I feel frustrated when I ask you to leave your brother alone and you don't listen. In the future, I'd like you to find another activity the first time I ask."

Also, observe the patterns of your family members. I know that by the time I get home from work, my wife is usually at the end of her rope. If I were to start complaining about my day or bringing up our budget, at the very least my comments would fall on deaf ears—and possibly result in a hostile response. The same applies to your children. My daughter Lauren is a morning person; she's ready and eager to talk as soon as she wakes. My sons, however, need about thirty minutes after waking up to figure out where they are. We all have periods during the day when we are more alert, calm, or withdrawn. Use your awareness of the patterns of others to help you select what you communicate and when.

Also, it's very important to talk openly about the issues your family is facing—not only feelings around an issue, but also plans for handling an issue, so that everyone is on the same page. If it's age-appropriate, consider asking your children for their suggestions for coping with an issue.

Advice from a Parent Who's Been There

Since my parents successfully kept our family intact despite the challenges of raising a child with autism, I asked my father what I should include in this section. He suggested focusing on the basics:

- Eat dinner together. Even if it's not always peaceful, eating dinner together can be the foundation of a family. Perhaps more important than the communication that occurs at dinner is the fact that you're all joined together as one entity—and it's visible to all of you that you are indeed together. During dinner together, let the answering machine pick up phone messages; if someone knocks on the door, don't answer.

- Have fun together. My parents took us on lots of walks. Walks are both free and good exercise. Try to schedule an activity to do together as a family every weekend. It doesn't have to be elaborate. Rent a video and make popcorn. Build a pillow fort. Go to the library.

- Identify behaviors that will not be tolerated by anyone in the family, under any circumstance. These should be behaviors that you're willing to go all the way to enforce. In my family growing up, we were absolutely not allowed to hit. Using drugs was outside the realm of possibility; none of us ever even considered it. Zero tolerance behaviors apply to everyone in the family and anyone who comes into your home.

- Communicate sincerely—your children will notice and appreciate your efforts. In other words, you don't have to communicate perfectly with each other; just commit to keep on doing your best.

My father finished by quoting Winston Churchill: "Never, never, never, never give up."

Personal Reflection

How would you describe your family's communication? Is it healthy and constructive? Does it go well most of the time, or is it often unsuccessful?

Can you think of ways to improve your family's communication? Do you have family time scheduled to talk about issues? Do you talk about your feelings and concerns or is there a lot of blame that shifts back and forth?

What activities do you do together as a family to have fun? How often do you have fun together as a family? Does everyone in the family know there are regular family times they can depend on?

What are the zero tolerance behaviors in your family? Does everyone know what will not be tolerated, and how these rules will be enforced?

How do you handle disagreements in your family, small and large? Is this method successful?

TALKING TO YOUR COMMUNITY

While it would make life much easier if the general population understood SPD, the reality is they don't yet. That's true for many disabilities. For example, while the general population may have a vague awareness of autism, it's extremely unlikely that a random stranger's assumptions will match the specific characteristics of your child with autism. One of the roles of your family is to replace these false assumptions with concrete, true examples.

It's important to understand the costs and benefits of communicating about your child's special needs with those outside your immediate family. You—and your children—should focus on communicating when the benefits outweigh the costs. Your children need to know that they don't have to explain SPD to everyone.

For example, while you may get odd looks in the grocery store because your child is humming loudly and rocking back and forth, you're probably not going to want to stop and explain SPD to everyone who gives your family an odd look—although the cost might be low, the benefit is even lower.

On the other hand, you might go to extensive lengths to communicate clearly with certain extended family members, particularly people whom you have a strong desire to maintain a positive relationship with. Although this scenario may involve a high cost, the benefit can also be high in the form of increased emotional support.

The Elevator Speech

You can also choose what depth of information you share. For situations in which you desire a low cost, quick approach, the *elevator speech* can be a particularly effective tool. The elevator speech is a traditional marketing tool—a short statement about your organization or a product or service that you provide targeted to the brief amount of time you're likely to spend in an elevator with a stranger. For the parent of a child with SPD, an elevator speech can be used to spark further conversation, satisfy curiosity, or just stop negative looks. Your elevator speech should both convey the essential elements of SPD and be easy to memorize.

My elevator speech goes something like this: "Sensory processing disorder is a disorder of the brain that affects the ability to make sense of sensory information from touch, taste, sound, smell, and sight." If the person asks for further information—usually who is affected—I then respond, "It affects about 5 percent of all school-age children. Many children with ADHD, autism, and learning disabilities also have sensory issues." It's up to you to determine how much information you want to provide.

Susan's elevator speech is a little different. It goes like this: "Aviva has sensory processing disorder. It affects the way she understands sensory information. It means she may rock her body or hum or slide off her chair, have trouble paying attention, and have difficulty with her balance and coordination. It's a neurological problem in her brain and she doesn't have control over these behaviors. She takes medications which help her a lot."

If, as a result of your elevator speech, people express interest in learning more about SPD, refer them to a Web site like the KID Foundation or the SPD Resources Web site connected to this book (see the resources section at the back of the book for contact information).

Beyond the Elevator Speech

There are many reasons for providing information well beyond the standard elevator speech, such as obtaining help, developing greater understanding, and establishing a friendship. You may also choose to go into more detail simply to help your child receive better care. In this situation, the same elements of effective communication apply; most notably, say what you mean and ask for what you need. If you're vague, or don't let people know what your needs are, they can't possibly help.

Beyond immediate practical reasons to communicate about your child's SPD at greater length, there's nothing so powerful as when someone understands our feelings, experiences, and identity as a human being. You can increase the odds of true understanding by sharing more detail; the greater the number of people you connect with, the better the chances are that you'll find someone who truly understands.

TALKING TO CARE PROVIDERS

Communicating effectively with care providers can be a challenge for any family. Even if we are able to access appropriate care, that care may not coincide with our cultural characteristics, beliefs, or values. In this country, we have a care system that's very prescriptive—it's sort of a this-is-the-way-it-is approach. Physicians hold such elevated status as experts that it can be very difficult to question them. And if we do raise concerns or provide feedback on the care our family is receiving, we may be regarded as a nuisance.

In order to better understand how to communicate with care providers, it's helpful to look at the experiences of one of the most disenfranchised populations in the United States. Whether you are Caucasian, African-American, Asian-American, or American Indian, there are many valuable lessons to be learned from the challenges that Hispanics have encountered in our country.

A Conversation with Jane Delgado

To understand the challenges faced by minority groups and apply these lessons to families with children with SPD, I spoke with Jane Delgado. Dr. Delgado is the president and CEO of the National Alliance for Hispanic Health, which provides services to over 12 million clients annually. She has received numerous awards and has served on many national boards, including the Patient Safety Institute and the National Advisory Council for Rosalyn Carter's task force on mental health. She is the author of *Salud!: A Latina's Guide to Total Health.*

A Cultural Perspective for Families of Children with Special Needs

I grew up in Brooklyn, New York, and now live in Washington, D.C., with my husband Mark and daughter Liz. I am a clinical psychologist by training. The last year of my training, I decided that while one-on-one therapy was meaningful, for some people you had to change institutions to truly improve their lives. Because of that, I went to Washington, D.C. to work in the U.S. Department of Health and Human Services and worked in the Office of the Secretary. After seven years of government service I joined the National Alliance for Hispanic Health and have just celebrated my twentieth anniversary at the National Alliance for Hispanic Health.

The Alliance is thirty-three years old. Our mission is to improve the health and well-being of Hispanics. We have four major centers: consumers, providers, science and policy, and technology. We also have a center for community services where we operate helplines where people can call us on our toll-free number [see the resources section at the back of the book for the Alliance's contact information] and we provide them with information about where they can go for services in their community. Any health information they want, we try to get to them . . .

It's interesting. [The Alliance is] supposed to be for the general Hispanic population, but we're finding that non-Hispanics are calling us because they find that we have a much more proactive, easier way to get information to them. So, even though it was originally intended just for Hispanics, we help anyone who calls.

. . . Our materials are easy to read in English or in Spanish. What happens is that a lot of people assume that the issues for Hispanics can be addressed through translation. Actually, translation is not enough, and, in fact, many of the materials that we are asked to translate into Spanish are pretty poor in English. Too often the materials in English are too complex—anybody who's under stress and trying to sort things out wants the information they need in an understandable and useable format.

You also have to consider the message that you are trying to communicate. The idea of parents as advocates is something that is not consistent with how Hispanic families function. A lot of the materials that are developed are done so with the concept that if you provide the information for advocacy, parents will be able to run with it. But that's like saying that Neiman Marcus has an open door and that anyone can come in. But not all people come in, because they think that store is not meant for them. Part of the challenge is helping people to accept advocacy as their right, and at the same time to also work to make the system more welcoming to them.

On matching programs to families' needs:

If you have a clinic that's not open at night, that makes it very hard for many working families—an appointment at certain hours means they have to lose precious hours of paid work. If you don't have people who understand the way different families operate and are open to that, it makes it unlikely that the family will feel welcome. This is also the situation if you have an organization that does not understand that faith and culture may be very important to a family.

Also, transportation plays a role. We did some surveys with low-income families. We found that while professionals talked about access, families talked about transportation. Sometimes, physically just getting to a place was difficult. If you think about some of the most successful programs—senior programs, Head Start—they often provide transportation. If you are a parent of more than one child, transportation is a big issue.

The way that materials are written can also be an issue. There is a national organization that we worked with in order to develop some materials. It was really a learning process for them, because they wanted to communicate in a way which was very directive, and not respectful. We said, "Well, you can't start there. You have to start with making the parent feel comfortable. One of the things you have to start thinking about is how to become a partner in making sure that the child gets the services they need, and what does this mean?" Eventually, you get to "And these are the things you can do." It is about starting at a different point in the process.

On communication and cultural proficiency:

Communication is basic—and is at the core of being welcoming. I always give the example of language. *Cultural competency* is when you know how to ask a question. *Cultural proficiency* is when you understand the answer. For example, very often, before people visit a foreign country they will teach themselves how to ask basic questions; e.g., "Where is the bathroom?" Unfortunately, when people answer, they have no idea of what is being said! Knowing how to ask a question is not going to get them where they need to go.

If you're going to make changes in someone's diet, or someone's home life, then you have to look at the reality in which the family lives. That's what being culturally proficient is all about. How does the family use their time? How do you get a parent to be involved if a parent is working all day and gets home exhausted because they're doing physical labor? What do you do when there's no child care available?

I remember being told once, "Well, Hispanics don't volunteer enough." I said, "Well, they don't volunteer because they're working sometimes more than two jobs." They're physically exhausted.

Also, Hispanics have the expectation of having an extended family. It's very important to us . . . it's what makes Hispanics strong. However, life in the United States, whether you're first generation or third generation, is often at odds with a construct where the family is central. Rugged individualism and all that it creates is not about nurturing your extended family . . .

Parents need to know that they have alternatives. Organizations should train parents about their options . . . Parents need specifics: these are some of the situations that come up and this is how you handle them. A brochure will not do it. It's more than giving parents or consumers a list of their rights and responsibilities. Parents need to develop skills, to see someone else doing them, and they need an opportunity to discuss the skills and their own hesitations.

Cultural proficiency is not just for Hispanics; it is how we treat each person. There have been some national surveys on language concordance in which 47 percent of Spanish-speaking patients reported that they had trouble communicating with their health care provider. These same surveys found that 18 percent of English-speaking non-Hispanics had trouble communicating with their health care provider. This is another example of the lack of cultural proficiency that is part of our system. Even those who speak the language of the system are having trouble being heard.

On the importance of advocacy conferences:

[These conferences offer] a very important opportunity. What happens at these conferences is people see role modeling. They discuss problems. They learn to become more comfortable challenging authority. They are able to see that there are other Hispanics who get their children the services they need and this encourages parents to learn the most effective ways to get more for their own children. Our respect for health and school professionals may sometimes make it difficult for parents to ask the tough questions . . .

Part of that is Hispanics' respect for authority and our tendency to be polite. These very positive attributes end up being attributes that make it unlikely that someone is going to challenge authority or act in a way which may be perceived as pushy. Yet, challenging authority is also about learning what is going on so you can get the best for your child. Challenging authority is not being pushy or being disrespectful, but rather trying to find what can be done, and being clear about it. We have to tell parents that it is okay not to know and so you have to be able to ask. It is good to tell parents, "Let us help you—these are things that you need to know about." We have found that among Hispanics, oftentimes people were not as attuned to what might be a symptom.

For example, in the area of depression, a family member may judge that the child who does not have the energy to work is just being lazy; or if there is something wrong with the child, maybe it's the diet. They may not consider that these are signs of something else going on. That's probably common with most parents as we want to believe that whatever is going on is manageable. The issue is what should parents do when the child is not being lazy and when it's more than a diet issue.

There is a stigma [attached to a diagnosis] and there is . . . the belief that what is occurring is manageable and will just go away because it is a temporary state. Remember that, as Hispanics are the least likely group to have health insurance, many parents may feel that because they don't have health insurance that there is no place where they can go for services. Generally, Hispanics try to take care of themselves. Parents let [symptoms] go without knowing that there are interventions that people can make to make the child's life much better and consequently make the family's life much easier.

Advice for parents:

First of all, understand that you are not alone. There are resources for parents to help their child and themselves.

There are professionals, parents, and organizations who want to help support you and your children. Too often, people think that their problems and those of their child are unique to them. That can be a very consuming thought.

In this culture, Hispanics very often feel alone. Too often even the media ignores Hispanics—except when there's some news about a drug bust or gang activity. And for a community where the concept of commmunity and family is important it is very, very hard. The parents of a special needs child must remember that they are not alone and there are organizations and people who want to be supportive.

I would encourage people to use the referral sources available through our helpline. The information specialist will be able to refer them to local services. Parents can reach out to local community-based organizations and social workers at hospitals—they are some of the kindest, most undervalued people. Parents need to know that they must reach out to other people.

Also, I think it's important to set limits with family members . . . You have to teach your family about the situation with your child. It is helpful for them and it also helps you. One of my friends has a child with cerebral palsy. When he was very small, people sometimes thought she was mean to him. She would make him sit at the table and eat as best he could. She explained, "He's not always going to be little. If he does things like that as a grown man, he won't have any friends."

. . . If you're Hispanic, African-American, Asian-American, or American Indian, you always stick out. Having a child with special needs makes it more obvious that you're different. Unfortunately, we're not at a point in our society where we celebrate differences. At best we still try to say everyone is the same and as a result end up suppressing the very differences that we need to acknowledge and celebrate.

The perspective to keep at the forefront is that every child needs a supportive environment and a community that helps that child grow to his or her fullest potential. We just have to understand that it's not going to be the same path or process for everyone. If you have a special needs child, you have to find the right environment for that child—just like you have to with every child.

—Jane Delgado
President and CEO of the National Alliance
for Hispanic Health

Lessons to Be Learned

Every organization has cultural biases, and sometimes these will or will not be congruent with our cultural beliefs. Each of us can learn from the experiences of other groups as they seek culturally proficient care. Furthermore, regardless of our color or faith, everyone benefits when care becomes more culturally proficient.

While there are many lessons to be learned from the conversation with Dr. Delgado, some key points are summarized below. (Some are my thoughts, based on our conversation, of how parents can address organizations.)

- Even though the health care system (or education system, mental health system, social services system, etc.) may not be welcoming, it's important to use the system for the well-being of your child.

- Professionals and organizations won't know how to meet your needs unless you identify and explain them. So, if a handout makes no sense because it's filled with medical jargon, let them know. Only parents know the unique issues of being a parent to their children. Don't leave it to professionals to guess at what you need.

- Being part of a community helps get your voice heard. There is an active community dedicated to the interests of families with children with SPD.

■ Challenging authority is not the same as being disrespect-ful or impolite.

■ It's okay for you to not know what to do and let profes-sionals help.

■ Parents are not alone. There are lots of resources to help your child and yourself.

■ Set limits with family members.

■ Every child develops better with a nurturing and support-ive environment, not just the child with special needs.

Your Cultural Identity

There was a time when I believed that I didn't have a culture. I seemed to just blend into society. I shared many of the values conveyed by the media—independence, timeliness, the importance of formal education, and materialism. I felt as though I didn't have a specific community to call home—I was envious of those who did. Through my work at the Mayor's Office for Education and Children in Denver, I've come to better understand the challenges encountered by minority groups and understand that we can have multiple cultural identities. I would now describe my culture as including experiences of my Christian faith, my European ancestry (specifically Scottish and German), my middle-class background, and a family heritage of public service.

There is both blessing and curse to the notion of cultural identity. First, there are many communities that we may be able to identify with and find support from; if we don't feel a strong connection, we may just need to go deeper into ourselves and that particular community. We can also change how we interact with our cultural identity. For example, if I can't draw the support I need from being Scottish, I can go deeper into my identity as a father instead.

The curse is that we may make incorrect assumptions based on our own cultural identity and experiences. I know I've made certain wrong assumptions in the past: I've assumed that everyone can go into a department store and be treated courteously; I've assumed that most people are able to get medical care when they need it. Closer to home, teachers may assume that because a child is in special education, she can't learn as well as her peers. Trouble occurs when assumptions interfere with our ability to communicate with and understand other groups.

During a workshop that my staff and I participated in, we were instructed to list all of the negative terms we heard growing up. Lists included nerd, dumb blonde, white trash, nigger, wetback, etc. As we looked around the room, we realized (some tearfully) that we were all described offensively on one list or another. Each of us could be labeled unfairly, and each of us had the potential to label others unfairly.

We all have emotional buttons that derive from our cultural experiences. These buttons can make it challenging for us to communicate effectively within our family and the community. In my culture, formal education is important and valued. If Brendan's teacher were to suggest that he couldn't learn as well as his peers, I'd flip. While what she might mean is that Brendan needs accommodations and extra support to learn as well as his peers (which I can live with), her initial statement would directly inflame one of my strongly held cultural values.

As another example, after we made the decision to place Brendan on medication, relatives continually questioned our judgment, in large part simply because of their own sets of cultural beliefs and values. Many of my in-laws are ranchers. Out on a ranch, you have to do everything yourself—sometimes even medical care. If an injury can't be seen, it doesn't exist. In this environment, a child with ADHD can be perceived as just needing more discipline; to have a child on medication for behavioral issues is just not done. For these relatives, the emotional button here came from a need to maintain independence from the health care system.

Personal Reflection

Before you can talk effectively to others, even to your own family, you need to be aware of what you think and feel about your own cultural identity. Think about your answers to the following questions in light of cultural values you may have. Are you afraid your child has a disability because of your parenting? Are you afraid questioning doctors would seem disrespectful? How does your cultural identity impact your caring for your child? Consider sharing your answers to the following questions with your spouse, if you feel comfortable in doing so.

How do you describe your cultural identity? Is it based primarily on religion, ethnic group, socioeconomic status, language group, or something else?

What traditions do you celebrate and why?

What were the values and beliefs of your family of origin? How did the parenting you received as a child relate to these values?

Growing up, did you have any friends or relatives with special needs? What were your thoughts and feelings about them and their circumstances?

Why do you think children have disabilities? What do your extended family and community believe?

Developing Parent and Professional Partnerships

The Parent Advocacy Coalition for Educational Rights (PACER Center)—created by parents of children and youth with disabilities to help other parents and families facing similar challenges— identifies five aspects to effective parent/professional collaboration:

Goals

The first is that both parties should have similar goals. Although the PACER Center suggests that the success of the child should be at the center of all goals that are developed, personally, I think the family as a whole should be at the center of every goal. Focusing exclusively on the child can lead to the neglect of the needs of others in the family. Professionals must understand that the health of the family is critical to the best outcome for the child. You want everyone working toward the same thing—a healthy family.

Respect

Parents and professionals need to show respect for each other. This doesn't mean that they have to agree. In fact, I would argue that courteously letting the other party know when you don't agree can be a way of showing respect. The foundation of respect is the understanding that people are doing the best that they can with the tools and resources that they have—whether they be parents or professionals.

Honesty

Honesty is critical to every relationship. If a particular therapy doesn't seem to be working—even if it's the tenth different therapy you've tried—let the therapist know. I have a chronic medical condition, as well as a particularly high resistance to medication. I've tried a wide variety of combinations to find something that works. Often, both my doctor and I would get discouraged and frustrated. Sometimes, I've felt so bad for my doctor that I wanted to tell him everything was great—even though it wasn't. In the end, if you aren't honest, your child and your family will suffer.

A Strengths-Based Approach

A strengths-based approach is appropriate for both professionals and parents. Professionals need to see and acknowledge the strengths of your family; it's more effective for professionals to build on preexisting strengths, rather than simply point out deficiencies. Similarly, professionals should also be recognized for *their* strengths, not blasted for their weaknesses. They're people too.

Hope

Parents and professionals also both need hope. Most professionals do what they do because they like to help people—they like to see successful outcomes. And parents often need reassurance that their family can be strong and supportive.

SUPPORT GROUPS

You may find joining a support group valuable for many reasons. For one thing, support groups allow you to become part of a larger voice. Our voices as parents need to be heard so the right messages are conveyed. We don't want professionals to just assume that they know what we need for our families. Only by banding together can we effectively share our needs with health care, education, mental health, and other systems.

Beyond that, support groups can be a great source of information. Want to know what a 504 plan is? Ask a parent who's been through the process. Dealing with feeding issues? (Many children with SPD have such issues.) Talk to other parents who've found strategies that work. Indeed, talking with other parents going through similar experiences can be a great source of emotional support.

One such support group is the KID Foundation's SPD Parent Connections. These support groups—found in most states—are run entirely by volunteer hosts. Although the national organization does share its resources with local support groups, each local host sets up a meeting schedule and handles all of the logistics of running the group—from advertising to finding speakers. Each host also maintains a lending library of donated books, videos, and CDs.

Parent to Parent groups can also be found in every state. Although these groups focus on disabilities in general as opposed to specifically SPD, these groups can still be a good source of information. The University of Kansas' Beach Center on Disability maintains a link to every Parent to Parent group in the country. (See the resources section at the back of the book for contact information.)

There are also listservs related to just about every disability that you can think of. The PACER Center maintains a good list of these resources (also listed in the resources section at the back of the book). If you don't find what you need there or through your own Internet searches, hop onto a listserv that's close to what you're looking for, and ask for a resource specifically targeted to what you need. Usually someone there will be able to point you in the right direction.

Personal Reflection

Is being part of a larger community important to you? What communities do you consider yourself a part of?

Do you feel that you are alone in dealing with your child?

What resources do you have available to you? (Resources may be financial, social, emotional, medical, or educational.)

How do you feel about challenging authority? About asserting your own knowledge of your child?

What parent/professional partnerships do you have? How well do you work with the therapists and others who help you with your child?

What kind of limits have you set with family members about giving you feedback/suggestions about how to care for your child? Do you need to set further limits?

_____

_____

FINAL THOUGHTS

Unfortunately, organizations often impose services on families without regard for what families want or need. Rather than avoid these organizations—and let our children and family suffer from lack of needed services or interventions—it's important to explain to those in these systems what is important to you and your family. Also, it's easy to feel alone parenting a child with SPD. The reality, however, is that there are many people out there—including other parents—who can help.

Chapter 7

Bringing Hope

Most of us, upon first hearing our child's diagnosis, go through common emotional stages. First, some of us refuse to believe it: "No, not our kid, she'll outgrow this, there's nothing wrong with her brain." Some get angry: "How could that happen to our son? We had good prenatal care, he has a healthy diet, no one in our family has ever had this before." Many of us then grow sad and depressed, afraid this means our child's life will be miserable and difficult—or that this situation is somehow our own fault. (Many parents of premature babies in particular experience strong feelings of guilt, convinced that something they did caused all of their child's problems.) Some of us also bargain with God, praying for our child to be normal in return for some sacrifice of our own. Until, at last, most parents get to acceptance, a stage of understanding that sensory processing disorder—or other disabilities—is simply part of who our child is, part of their specialness, part of what we can love and cherish about them.

In this chapter, I (Susan) will explain how to bring hope and promise back into your life—and into the life of your child with SPD. In some ways, this chapter may be the most important of the book: If we do not have hope, we cannot maintain the positive outlook on the future that we and our child deserve.

Think of the stress your family is experiencing. You've had the shock of the diagnosis, and perhaps, like me, premature birth as well. Medical bills can easily be overwhelming and finding the right therapists is often frustrating and difficult. Your extended family may not be supportive of your struggles. We've already talked about coping with the strain on your marriage, on typically-developing siblings, and on your relationships with your extended family and your community. Now we'll focus on both how to cope with the fact that your child may not have the life you had hoped for, and how to adjust your expectations of who your child is and who she may become.

RISK AND PROTECTIVE FACTORS

When your child enters the disability or special education world, you hear the phrase "at risk" a lot. Children are considered at risk for learning problems because of risk factors such as premature birth. (In fact, premature birth tends to make it more likely children will have multiple problems later on, because preemies are also more likely to have other risk factors—including severe respiratory difficulties at birth or complications at delivery—and premature birth itself is also more likely to occur in poorer people, which also raises the risk of later learning problems for other reasons.) Children may also be at risk for illnesses because of neurological or medical conditions, or at risk for educational failure because of learning problems.

When children are at risk, you also tend to hear the term "resilience." Researchers define *resilience* as a "process of, or capacity for, or the outcome of, successful adaptation despite challenging and threatening circumstances" (Garmezy and Masten 1991). Or, in other words, a resilient person does well despite a bad—or even terrible—situation.

The Web site of the American Psychological Association offers this definition of resilience: "Resilience is the process of adapting well in the face of adversity, trauma, tragedy, threats, or even significant sources of stress—such as family and relationship problems, serious health problems, or workplace and financial stressors. It means 'bouncing back' from difficult experiences."

Thus, although children may be at risk for problems because of neurological, medical, or learning conditions, the impact of these risk factors may be lessened by the resilience of the child—the natural ability of the child to bounce back.

I find this immensely hopeful—our children aren't necessarily fated by their disorders to live hard lives; rather, they have the possibility to adapt, recover, and rise above their difficulties. Being the goal-directed person I am, after I learned about the importance of resilience, I immediately wanted to find out how I could help my daughter become as resilient as possible. Unfortunately, it's not quite that simple.

PARADIGM SHIFTS

Before we can help our children become more resilient we have to make some paradigm shifts. A *paradigm* is an example that serves as a pattern or model for something. We have paradigms for most things in our lives—how we behave toward one another, how schools are supposed to be organized, how we should be treated at our jobs, and how we think about our children. The well-known author Steven Covey in his well-known book *The Seven Habits of Highly Effective People* (1989) described a paradigm as a map inlaid in the mind that determines the way you see the world. Researchers Wolin and Wolin (1997) explain that paradigms are developed by our personality, how we were brought up, our family, friends, colleagues, schooling, and work environment. We seldom think about our paradigms. Rather, we accept them without question. Indeed, what *you* accept as a paradigm usually supersedes your acceptance of other people's realities. When contradictions arise in an encounter with someone else's paradigm, these contradictions tend to be dismissed as inaccuracies, misperceptions, or mistakes. The whole process repeats itself again and again without our even noticing.

The first paradigm shift we need to make to change the way we see our kids is in our language. Think about the phrases below:

Disabled kids

Children with special needs

Handicapped children

Children with autism

In the second and last phrases, the children come first and the disability is simply a descriptive detail, like brown hair or blue eyes. In the others, the disability is the defining characteristic, the way the child is viewed in the eyes of the world. The former is called *person first language*, and it's an important start to talking differently about our children. Yes, it's true, their special issues are a part of them, but maybe not the most important part of them. Just talking differently about our children and their disabilities can shift our thinking about them. When we describe our children to others by stating their disabilities first, these disabilities then define the first impression others have of them. All other impressions are filtered through that one. While some people may still be able to see our child accurately, many will develop a distorted view instead—they'll assume our child is stupid or slow or unable to accomplish things because they're blind or autistic or have ADHD.

The second necessary paradigm shift is in our labels. I've struggled over the years with whether to tell people about Aviva's disabilities or not. She doesn't look disabled to others, but given enough time her behavior will mark her as different. She hums, rocks her body, and chews on her hand—and is completely oblivious to all of it. If you tell her to stop, she will. For a moment. Then she'll start again, and when you tell her to stop again, she'll be truly surprised—she has no idea she's even doing the behavior. She's simply soothing herself. (When I have to tell her to stop for the third or fourth time, I get as annoyed as anyone, by the way.) I've finally chosen to tell others about her disabilities on a regular basis, to spare them—and her—the aggravation of these encounters. If I warn others that Aviva doesn't know she's doing these things, they're less likely to assume that she's doing them on purpose to annoy them. But I don't start by saying, "This is my disabled daughter." I say, "This is Aviva. She has sensory processing disorder, which means she has trouble handling some sensory information. She may rock or hum, but she doesn't know she's doing it. Just ask her to stop if it bothers you." I can see the change in the way they look at her, and I feel better about everyone's understanding of the situation.

Another obstacle to changing the way we think about our kids is that our school and health care systems require us to label our child's problems prominently in order to get the help and support our child needs. If a doctor keeps describing our child as a problem, we often fall into the habit as well. It's hard to resist that authority. Initially I always started my descriptions of Aviva by emphasizing the things she didn't or couldn't do—she didn't roll over, she didn't crawl or walk on time, she didn't speak or babble as she should have, she had very damaged lungs and one eye with damaged sight. Although emphasizing these things was useful in some ways—it helped me to get her physical and occupational therapy, speech therapy and music therapy, and trips to the pulmonologist and ophthalmologist, mostly paid for by insurance or by Part C, the federally funded early intervention program—its side effect was that it continually reminded us of how at risk Aviva was, how damaged and how disabled.

Unfortunately, the paradigm that a disability is a problem to be treated—and that as a result our children must be at risk for more problems—is very hard to change. The at-risk paradigm is a major part of the way people view children with special needs. Doctors, teachers, nurses, therapists—even us, the parents—all assume that because our children experience some type of difficulties, other problems will also occur. The resilience paradigm isn't easy to accept either. It can be hard for parents to overcome their view of their child as at risk—and see the child instead as having a natural ability to accept difficult situations, recover from them, and move on.

A Conversation with Kathy Marshall

To better understand the concept of resilience, Chris and I spoke to Kathy Marshall of the National Resilience Resource Center at the University of Minnesota.

A Child "At Promise"

I think what's important for parents to understand is that every person—regardless of circumstance, regardless of personal condition—actually has what I would call a *natural resilience*. It is our birthright as human beings. It means that at the very core there is the capacity to navigate life well.

[Focusing on resilience] means a major change in how professionals, families, children, and teenagers, actually see the situation we might call a disability. We have a choice to make: Do we see an individual as "at risk" or "at promise?" That view that you hold of your child absolutely either diminishes or enhances the chances your child will do well . . .

The medical model and the specialized labeling process have probably forced you to have to say [these are the needs, this is the disability] to get services. But almost no one's happy with putting a child in a negative box . . . Even though a child has a diagnosis and dollars flow and programs are planned on the basis of that diagnosis, the real issue is that somehow—and it begins in the home I think—somebody has got to bring *hope* into the picture. Not hope that the diagnosis is wrong or will go away, but hope that, in addition to that challenged part of that child's being, there is also a healthy whole part. It may show up in the slightest touch or it may show up in a humorous encounter where everybody ends up laughing, or as grades that were never supposed to happen.

The truth is, this whole process of special education and diagnosis is a very young profession and we don't know very much. We really don't know how a child can do amazing things and still have all of these disabilities. Every person, regardless of their relationship with their child, has stories to tell about when they have been surprised or noticed something outstanding or meaningful or touching or worthwhile or successful that a child with a disability has done or is able to do. It may be as simple, in very severe cases, as the individual child being, for a moment, quiet and calm. Or it may show up as a smile or a touch that communicates a connection with another person. Or it may be very, very dramatic.

Resilience is an innate capacity we are born with and we die with. It's not time-bound . . . [It's important to recognize this capacity in our children.] You need to live in the moment and be healthy and unattached to blind spots so you can see fresh, right then and there what is strong and promising about your child. Don't run this into your intellect. Rather, you want to genuinely trust that there's more capacity in an individual than there's lack of capacity.

Advice for encouraging resilience in parents:

I would suggest that parents pay attention to when they are experiencing a good feeling. You may be surprised that you even have some good feelings given all you are going through. Trust your mind to make it apparent to you how that good feeling happened . . . Don't try to figure it out. Let it be and trust the process. Your common sense, natural resilience, and wisdom will guide you effortlessly . . .

[Focusing on the good feelings can encourage resilience.] Let's say I had a nice feeling with my child when we were sitting by a window and we were watching a sunset; maybe in that moment I wasn't thinking about much, but my heart sure was connected to my little one. (Just recognizing this feeling will allow you to notice good feelings more often in the future.) The next morning your child may be saying a lot of stuff that you could potentially fire back at. Instead, you can remember that feeling of sitting by the window and say to yourself, "You know, I think I'm going to just be for a minute." Maybe the child even catches a little sense of that. At least you do. At a minimum, you don't get into huge arguments—and you hold onto your own peace of mind.

—Kathy Marshall
   Executive Director, National Resilience Resource Center
   University of Minnesota

When I first called Kathy to discuss the possibility of her contributing to this book, she asked me an amazing question. She asked me if there had been a moment in my daughter's life when I suddenly saw her completely differently. Without hesitation, I answered yes. It happened just after Aviva's sixth birthday, the day before Aviva's scheduled triennial IEP meeting (an evaluation of the need for special education services that the school district performs every three years). The school psychologist stopped me on the playground and asked me to come and speak to her. I immediately thought something was wrong.

When we went into her office, the psychologist told me two very important and contradictory things: First, Aviva had a thirty-three point difference between her verbal and nonverbal scores on the intelligence test, which meant she had a learning disability. Second, her scores were high enough to qualify her for the Denver Public Schools Gifted and Talented Program and, later, which magnet program would I like to send her to?

I burst into tears. My one-pound-eleven-ounce micro-preemie, who hadn't rolled over, crawled, walked, talked, or seen properly, would go to a school for the gifted! It totally turned my world upside down. I had always described Aviva in terms of what she couldn't do, in terms of what she needed help with, in terms of what her limits were. Now I had to get used to describing her strengths and her skills.

This was my moment of paradigm shift. Because of that one moment of realization of Aviva's strengths, I will never see her the same way again. Even though the psychologist told me in that same meeting that Aviva had a significant learning disability—one for which we have had to arrange many accommodations and therapies ever since—the moment I really remember, deep down inside, is the moment she told me that Aviva was gifted.

Personal Reflection

Has there been a moment in your child's life when you suddenly saw your child completely differently? Remember all the details of that moment.

Sit quietly for a few minutes and recall a shared moment with your child that was positive and special.

Reflect on some skill or ability your child has, no matter how small. When did you first see this skill or ability? How do you help your child use this skill or ability?

Seeing my child as "at promise" instead of at risk doesn't mean she doesn't need therapy and support. Aviva has a rare and complex learning disability; she will continue to need accommodations and modifications in school, help with organization at home, assistive technology such as a computer for typing her work, and social skills training to help her learn to interact with others. What my paradigm shift does mean, however, is that I now also see Aviva's strengths and natural resilience as resources that will be there for her as her life goes on.

SUPPORTING YOUR CHILD'S NATURAL RESILIENCE

Although natural resilience develops as part of daily life, researchers in the area of resilience also believe that we can help reinforce children's natural strengths by offering them supports in a variety of areas.

Cognition

First, be aware of your child's cognitive—or thinking—skills. Expose your child to a wide variety of information. We all know reading is important, but so are objects and environments. Children love zoos and museums not just for the tigers and dinosaur bones, but because zoos and museums stimulate imaginations.

Children with SPD may do best in places where they can experience the world through different senses. Recently the Denver Museum of Nature and Science hosted a "Grossology" exhibit—an exhibit that allowed children to explore the particularly gross nature of our bodily functions. This type of exhibit can be a huge success for children who are sensory-seeking, but something to be avoided for sensory-avoidant children. Use what you have learned about the subtypes of SPD to find the right environments to support your child's learning. In the right sensory environment, your child may be capable of much more effective learning.

For example, Aviva uses a weighted belt to help her stay in her seat during longer writing assignments, and she has a rubber elastic bracelet to chew on if she feels the need for more stimulation. She can also ask to leave the room to do relaxation techniques if frustration or anxiety is making it hard for her to concentrate. These are all techniques she has learned to call on when her natural ability to observe herself tells her that her learning is being interrupted by her negative feelings.

Autonomy

Autonomy is the ability to accomplish tasks on one's own. People who are autonomous think for themselves and make their own decisions. It's easy to assume that children with SPD aren't capable of being autonomous, but this assumption is wrong. In fact, we may simply need to teach them different strategies to accomplish this goal. For our family, Aviva's particular learning disability makes this goal especially challenging. Sometimes my husband and I will assume that she's not capable of doing tasks for herself and do them for her, when the reality is that we just don't want to do the work that it would take to help her do the task on her own. Recently, on a listserv I belong to, a woman was writing at length about problems she was experiencing with her thirteen-year-old son, and casually mentioned that she had to stop work to make him a sandwich for lunch. I was surprised. I immediately wrote her and asked why he couldn't do this himself. She was equally surprised. She had always done this for him because when he was having a bad day, he needed a tremendous amount of support to do it himself.

By assuming our children have the natural promise to achieve what they want to achieve, we can make it more likely that they will learn to act independently and learn to take care of themselves independently as well. This doesn't necessarily mean more work—it may just mean that we need to take a different attitude or hold different expectations about what our child can do.

Social Skills

At its core, having good social skills simply means being able to understand and have relationships with others. Good social skills help children be more successful in many situations, including family, school, and their community. However, for many children with special needs, social skills are difficult.

Richard Lavoie (1994) has written extensively about children with learning disabilities, including several articles focused on social skills. The following are some of his suggestions for helping a child struggling with social skills:

- Observe your child in a wide variety of social situations to really understand how they behave and interact with others.

- Develop some easy-to-use and easy-to-remember signals to help your child get out of difficult situations. For example, if your child asks too many questions without letting others answer, arrange to touch your ear in a certain way. Then, when your child sees your signal, they'll know to keep quiet and let someone answer a question.

- Enroll your child in group activities and events specifically targeted to your child's interests and abilities.

- Establish a reward system to reinforce any small or large social successes.

- Get all family members involved in supporting your child's social success, including siblings.

- When watching television or movies—or when seeing other kids and families interact—be sure to talk with your child about the behaviors and choices they are seeing. It will help them understand what others are doing.

There are many excellent resources on social skills available (you'll find some of them in the resources section at the back of this book). For now, the key point to remember is that your child is capable of reaching out and forming good relationships with your help and support.

Feelings of Internal Control

For many people, a belief that they have control over the decisions and events in their lives is a source of self-esteem and strength. When you believe you can influence your own fate and control your own life choices, you believe you can achieve what you wish.

The drive for internal control begins early; for example, when infants throw everything they can on the floor, they're exercising their sense of control. And when toddlers insist on dressing themselves— even though it takes all day—they're exercising their sense of control. We want to encourage these feelings of internal control in our children as part of their natural sense of resilience. We can accomplish this in part by rewarding them when they have completed a task on their own and showing them how they relied on their own skills and abilities to achieve the outcome.

FINAL THOUGHTS

We all need to bring hope and promise back into our lives. Learning to live with a child with special needs can be stressful and difficult and depressing and exhausting. (I'm sure you can think of other negative adjectives I've forgotten to include!) But we must stop dwelling on the negative and remember our natural promise and the natural promise of our children. We all have the capacity to think, observe, learn, bounce back, and succeed, each in our own way. Our job, as parents of our special children, is to speak of them and to them in ways that support these capacities. We all possess a natural resilience.

I challenge you to take time in the next days and weeks to just be with your child. Share the good feelings of seeing your child's promise. Remember those feelings. Let that hope be with you during the harder times that we all face with our children.

Chapter 8

Making It Happen—
Building a Healthy Family

The foundation has been laid. You now have tools to support your marriage and all of your children. You have an understanding of SPD, and know how to talk about it, both within your family and within your community. You know, too, how to nurture and build upon the natural resiliency inherent in your children and your family.

All of this knowledge can be a powerful support for your family and your child with SPD. Family is probably the most significant positive or negative influence in a child's life. Your child will find it easier to tackle tough challenges at school and in the community because she knows that there's a safe haven at home. By watching you, your child will learn how to nurture and enjoy healthy relationships. These skills will then transfer to your child's children and so on. How, then, do we put all of this knowledge into practice, and build the healthy family we desire?

The answer lies in coupling the broad knowledge that you have gained thus far with the ability to handle the details of daily life. The skills that you already have—among others, nurturing relationships and communicating effectively—will certainly make it easier to handle the details. In this chapter, however, we'll look more closely at the day-to-day issues as well as practical strategies for daily living. These strategies include ways to handle daily stress, make effective decisions, and manage scarce monetary resources.

The simple stresses of living can easily throw a family off track. For example, a couple of weeks ago, I noticed a bulge in the drywall in our basement. I touched it—my finger sank into wet paste. The next day we called a plumber. Initially, the estimate was $350. However, once the plumber got into the wall, he discovered the leak was actually much higher, from the kitchen above. The price also went much higher. When all was said and done, we were faced with a $2,000 plumbing bill, ruined carpet, and gaping holes in our wall. Add in the everyday challenges of parenting a child with SPD, and this type of situation has the potential to send anyone over the edge.

HOW TO HANDLE THE STRESS

Many books have been written on coping with stress; several good ones are listed in the resources section at the back of this book. I'll just cover the highlights here. Based on my family's experience and the experience of families I know, I came up with what I believe are five major factors in managing stress. (You'll create a list specific to the individual characteristics of your family later in the chapter.)

Stress Relievers

1. Obtain regular respite.

2. Practice some form of spirituality.

3. Nurture your relationships.

4. Live in the moment.

5. Appreciate the little things.

Respite

Let's start with respite. A *respite* is a brief interval of rest and recovery—but in many ways, respite is just a fancy professional term for child care. Parents must have breaks now and then. Unfortunately, unless your child has a significant disability, it's unlikely that you'll have your respite paid for by any agency. Most likely, you're on your own. While it would be great to have a nanny, few of us can afford that. Even the teenage babysitter down the street can put a dent in your budget. Going out to dinner can easily cost $50, plus another $30 for the sitter. Few families I know can afford to do that every week.

What, then, are your options? If you live reasonably close to a university, you could contact the education, counseling, or occupational therapy program and ask if any students need practicum hours. Typically, these students need such hours to get licensure. Working with your child with SPD can give students great experience. In return, you may be able to get free or lower-cost child care.

Other more traditional approaches include asking relatives to help, trading time with friends who have children with similar needs, or joining a babysitting cooperative. Babysitting cooperatives can be anything between formal memberships and informal arrangements between friends. Typically, you agree to take in children from other families in the cooperative at times that are convenient to you. These hours are then banked. Banked hours can be used to have other families watch your children on an hour-for-hour basis. Cooperatives are usually discovered by word of mouth. The best people to ask are your friends. Other good places to inquire are your church, regular day care provider, and your child's school.

Practice Spirituality

There is a general agreement among researchers that those who have some form of religious or spiritual faith are healthier and often happier. They have better marriages and report being more satisfied with their lives. Spirituality can give us a sense of purpose, structure, social support, and an appreciation of humankind. I'm not advocating for any particular form or practice of spiritual or religious belief; I only want you to consider the importance of having some form of faith in your life—research shows that practicing some form of spirituality is good for the emotional health of everyone in a family.

Nurture Relationships

When you have the support of a loved one, it's like having an army on your side; challenges are much easier to handle. Chapter 3 presented some practical strategies to strengthen your relationship with your spouse. But other relationships are critical too. Extended family can be an important source of support. Older relatives in particular also offer different perspectives and the wisdom of greater experience.

Your friends are also extremely valuable. The need for friends doesn't end after high school or college. While it's easy to devote all of your time to your spouse and children, you—and your family, too—will be happier if you have a network of friends. Nurturing and maintaining friendships does take time. You'll probably need to plan ahead with your spouse or relatives so that you have time for these relationships. If it's difficult to arrange, it's also sometimes possible to combine friends and family. Invite another family over for dinner or dessert. Meet at a park or go swimming together.

Live in the Moment

Living in the moment means letting life unfold as it happens. Rather than thinking about the past or future or what should be, focus on what is happening now. For example, it's easy to find yourself wishing that your child were a typically-developing child without many challenging behaviors. However, as easy as that thought is, it's also likely to bring up anxiety about the future—or perhaps feelings of regret for the past. And while you're engaged with this painful emotional trip, you're missing the opportunity to be with your child.

It's difficult to live in the moment. Every second of the day, a multitude of thoughts swarm around in your head. Each of these thoughts has the potential to take you on an emotional ride. For example, seeing things scattered on the floor might remind you of all of the times that you've had to pick up for someone else. This flood of thought might then bring up resentment or even anger. This anger can then show up in how you talk to members of your family, which might irritate and provoke them, too. Soon, that little trigger of seeing things lying on the floor has taken a toll on the emotions of everyone in the house.

To live in the moment takes practice and awareness. Many find that meditation helps free the mind. Journaling is another good way to both let go of your thoughts and reframe negative thoughts into positive ones. Everyone has untapped strength inside. All we need to do is focus on the present and pay attention to our intuition and feelings.

The goal is to be able to live freely and take life as it unfolds. This doesn't mean that you have to be passive, however. Trust your common sense and allow your knowledge of what is right for you and your family to guide your actions.

Appreciate the Little Things

In our society, it can be very difficult to appreciate what we have. Every day, we are bombarded with messages telling us that what we have isn't good enough. We need the newest, latest model; we need something bigger, fancier, more prestigious. At work, there's often continuous quality improvement—which can easily make you feel that whatever work you've done up to now isn't good enough.

What's missing is the appreciation for what we have, how far we have come, and the small successes on the way. Brendan struggles with reading. If we were to measure him by where he should be in his reading, both he and I would be discouraged. Yet, the other day he brought home his daily sticker chart, and had earned a sticker for good behavior and accomplishment for every period of the day. For Brendan, that's an enormous achievement! Appreciating the little things means observing the challenges that your child has overcome—large and small—and recognizing these achievements. Maybe your child dressed herself that morning. Maybe your child ate most of dinner without any major fuss.

Appreciating the little things also means realizing that at any moment we could lose everything that we have. All that you have is a gift. Sure, maybe the carpet in your house is dirty, but at least you have carpet and not a dirt floor. If you've got a roof over your family, enough food to eat, and adequate medical care, you've done very well.

Take the time to appreciate the small things in your life on a daily basis. Did your child's clothes match today? Did you all get out the door on time? Was dinner on the table at a reasonable hour and were all of you there to eat it? If so, you had a day worth appreciating.

A Conversation with a Parent of a Child with Special Needs

Rhonda Williams has an unusual cultural background. She is a mixture of African-American and American Indian (Lakota Sioux) and was raised with traditional American Indian values. She speaks Lakota fluently. She brings a unique perspective to coping with significant life challenges as well as the daily stress of parenting a special needs child in a blended family. Rhonda's story shows how both spirituality and culture can be sources of support.

Rhonda's experience combines many elements: being a member of a minority group, raising a blended family, dismal health care, loss,

---

Finding Peace in the Midst of Stress

I'm married and we have a blended family—four girls and one boy. My stepdaughter Amber has ADHD. She has lived with us since she was seven years old . . .

I had a daughter who passed away at seven months of age. She was diagnosed with a congenital heart defect that was a result of having Down syndrome. She wasn't diagnosed as having Down syndrome until we brought her from the reservation in South Dakota to the Children's Hospital in Denver . . . After she passed away, I went to speak with her pediatrician on the reservation. I asked him how they missed this at birth. His reply to me was that a lot of African-American children and American Indian children look mongoloid anyway. He said it was hard for them to diagnose. It never entered their mind.

On being a stepmother of a child with special needs:

I think educators and the school that Amber went to looked at me as an outsider—the stepmother—even though I adopted her. Amber is light-skinned with light brown hair and green eyes. *[Rhonda has very dark skin.]* That was a challenge because when I went to meet with the teachers, they would get this weird look on their face, like, "Do *you* have the right to make decisions about Amber?"

Before we had a diagnosis . . . Amber was labeled in school as a bad child, a troublemaker. The school got into a habit of calling about every little behavior she had in school. Trying to work and take care of that after a while gets really stressful. I'm just lucky that I had really understanding employers. My husband did, too. We alternated every week on whose turn it was to deal with the school.

On managing daily stress:

I do a lot of meditating. I attend sweat lodges at least once or twice a month. I take a lot of walks or I sit in my backyard. I think it's important to take time for you. I do a lot of reading around spirituality and spiritual ways to take care of myself . . .

[I'm] grounded by the practices of Lakota people, the spiritual principles that I was brought up with. I've had a lot of support through my family and the reservation. My cousin is a Yuwipi man. I guess you could equate that to a medicine man. He is really supportive and I can call him when I'm feeling overwhelmed or stressed out. He helps me get grounded back in myself.

Advice for readers:

It's important to have a cultural group that you identify with. I think that is *so* important—because sometimes you can say, "Why me, God?" and get into a place where you're losing yourself with all the stress going on. It's also important to find something that you're passionate about—whether it's exercise or meditation or yoga. You also need to know who you are, not only internally, but also physically. I think it helps to be totally aware of your body so that you know when to turn off the switch and take some time to yourself. Know what those red flags of stress are, or when you're feeling overloaded.

—Rhonda Williams
   Professional family advocate
   Stepmother of a child with special needs

and parenting a child with special needs. Through all of the stresses, Rhonda has embraced her unique cultural identity and drawn strength from it, allowing her to raise her family successfully. Amber is now seventeen, a senior in high school in the process of applying to college. She has friends and has done well academically.

There are many different ways to deal with stress. Here are some suggestions:

- Share the workload—both at home and at work—with everyone.

- Have family friends and arrange playdates for your children.

- Celebrate successes, big or small—everyone loves parties!

- Exercise together as a family—take walks, go for a bike ride, play catch.

- Have a family pet.

- Read; it doesn't matter what—comics, literature, or the newspaper.

- Watch the sunset.

- Get a massage or a manicure—or give your partner a back rub or foot rub.

- Have a hobby—do needlepoint, fix cars, garden, build stuff, etc.

- Play video games.

Personal Reflection

Make a list of ten things you can do to relieve stress. Rank them in order. Think about the top five factors we've explored—respite, spirituality, relationships, living in the moment, and appreciating the little things—and include the ones you think belong on your list. Think of strategies to be sure you can get three to five of these stress relievers every week—then do them!

What do you do for respite? Do you receive enough respite to maintain a healthy spirit? If not, how can you get what you need?

What does spirituality or faith mean to you? To your partner? Have you talked about these issues together?

What do you appreciate most about your network of friends? If your network isn't as extensive as you'd like, what steps can you take to expand it?

What does living in the moment mean to you? How can you live more in the moment?

What do you appreciate most about your family? What do you appreciate most about your life? How can you be more appreciative of the little things?

MAKING DECISIONS

All parents have to make tough decisions on a regular basis, from setting budgets to choosing schools, from arranging child care to balancing work and family. Parents of children with special needs have to make even more decisions—and decisions with potentially lasting consequences. Sometimes, parents will also need to keep making decisions for their child with special needs for the rest of their lives.

When Brendan went through a medication change, his behavior got so out of control that his psychiatrist suggested we have him hospitalized. If you read the chapter on siblings, you'll know that for me this seemed as though history was repeating itself. This was a very difficult, emotional decision to make. Should we try to contain him at home—even though he was hurting everyone in the family—or should we get him stabilized in the hospital? Eventually we chose (as my parents did with my brother) to keep him at home, with his family.

Another decision you may have to make for a child with SPD is whether the special education system is the best route for your child, or whether it might be better to keep your child out of special education and provide your own system of supports instead. You may need to decide whether to put your child on medication or not. Also, how best to balance the needs of your child with SPD with the needs of the rest of the family.

We've already explored some of the tough decisions that you'll need to make—decisions about relationships, communication, providing support to siblings, involving fathers, and leading your family. For each of these topics, you've also had opportunities for personal reflection—which will help you make your decisions. In this section, we're going to talk in more detail about the process of making decisions, and how you can develop a process that is specific to the needs of your family.

Establishing a Foundation for Decision Making

Regardless of your cultural background, the most crucial brick in the foundation of your decision-making process is a clear understanding of your values, and the values of your family. Every decision needs to be made in the context of your values as a family. If a decision is made that conflicts with your values, the decision cannot have a positive outcome. It cannot last. In chapter 2, we talked about values in terms of parent leadership. Every parent and every family should understand the glue that keeps it together. Your values could be based on religion, social justice principles, or just the importance of family. Values are what you hold to be true; values are reflected in your daily actions as a family.

Another brick in the foundation of your decision-making process is knowing who makes the final decision. Part of this is knowing when, as parents, you or your partner need to make an executive decision and when you need to involve the entire family. Another part of this is making it clear to everyone whether you're gathering input but will make the final decision yourselves, or if everyone will participate in making the final decision.

As parents, you may need to make executive decisions in cases where the safety and security of your family is at stake. In these cases, there shouldn't be any negotiation—your decision is final and everyone needs to comply with what you have decided. You may also need to make an executive decision if there's dissension in the family and reaching a consensus isn't critical. For example, choosing a restaurant for dinner—if there are arguments, you or your partner may simply want to put your foot down and make a decision.

Consistency is critical. If you have reached a decision, stick to your decision until either a positive outcome is reached, or clear evidence indicates that another course of action is needed. This also means that as a couple, you and your partner make decisions together and present a united front. If there is resistance to your decision from other family members, you need to stick together and hold tight. If evidence indicates that another course of action is needed, make it clear that as a couple, you have determined to change direction and that another decision needs to be made in order to reach a positive outcome.

The last brick in the foundation is to sit back and wait to make a decision until you have a clear mind. This is when your natural resilience (discussed in chapter 7) comes into play. We can tap into this natural resilience when we notice good feelings, live in the moment, and observe ourselves and our surroundings. Find a sense of peace and trust that you will know what to do when the time is right. Sometimes the best decision is not to make a decision.

Establishing a Process for Making Decisions

On top of the foundation described above, each family builds its own process for making decisions, a process that reflects that family's own cultural background, family of origin, and values. The questions in this section will help you define a process that is unique to your family. We'll look first at your family of origin and cultural background to see how these influences may impact the process that you establish, and then at the process that you currently have in your family and explore whether this process may need to be refined.

The Decision-Making Process and Your Expectations

1. In your family of origin, who made final decisions? Was it your parents together, an extended family member, or one of your parents?

2. In the culture that you identify with, who is traditionally the final decision maker in the family?

3. When you got married, who did you think would be the decision maker?

4. In your culture, what is the traditional process for making decisions? Do children have any input? Are extended relatives involved in the process, and if so, how?

5. How are the answers to these questions reflected in your own family?

In order to understand the process your family has now, it's important to understand the biases you started with. This can help you understand the challenges that your family faces in making decisions. You may have different biases than your partner. For example, you may want to gather input from your children and extended family, while your partner believes that decision making should only involve the parents. If you understand the origin of the disagreement, it's easier to communicate about the issue and come to some form of resolution.

The next set of questions focuses on the process your family currently uses to reach decisions. (As we've discussed, the process may be different in different circumstances.) First, you want to understand the general approach your family takes to make decisions. Only then can you determine whether this approach reflects your values—and ultimately if it's working.

Your Current Decision-Making Process

1. When faced with a tough decision (choosing a school or course of therapy, addressing important medical issues, etc.), how does your family reach a decision?

2. Do you gather input from extended relatives, friends, or your children?

3. How important is it that you have consensus in your family?

4. What was your family's experience the last time you had to make a difficult choice?

Compare your answers to the first set of questions to your answers to the last set. Are your cultural beliefs and traits of your family of origin reflected in your current process? It's okay if your answers don't match—as long as you are truly comfortable with the process that you have now. If you aren't comfortable with the process that you currently have, identify the value or element of your family of origin or culture that's missing from your current process. It could be that you and your partner have different beliefs about who should be involved. If that's the case, use the skills in chapter 3 to discuss what's important to you, and how you can get your needs met. The process that you develop will break down on occasion. That's okay. Start again and keep practicing and communicating.

Lastly, take another look at your foundation for decision making, and compare this with your family's process. I would argue that it's important to be consistent, to know who is involved in decision making, and to recognize that you don't have to make decisions if you're not ready. However, your family may not embrace each of these elements. If that's the case, then what would you say is the foundation of your family's decision-making process? What were the influences on your foundation?

Evaluating Decisions

How you evaluate the results of your decisions depends on your personality profile. Some people are very data oriented. They want to see hard facts that indicate whether a decision is working or not. These people often love the technical aspects of analyzing results—for example, charting frequency, duration, and intensity of behaviors.

Others prefer to just observe and trust their instincts. They may evaluate the results of a decision based on their own feelings, or they may seek anecdotal evidence—for example, does the child seem happier?

Neither approach is right or wrong; they're just different. Personally, I fall somewhere in the middle. I'm not wild about data, but I do like to have more tangible evidence than just feelings and perceptions. The way to bridge these differences is to make it clear from the beginning how you will measure the outcome of your decision. I recommend that you make your evaluation method as simple as possible. If you are data driven and your partner is not, you may want to consider looking at different aspects of the outcome in order to get a complete picture.

For example, when my wife and I were deciding whether to keep Brendan at home or have him hospitalized, we measured the outcome of our decision very differently. My wife kept a chart of how many tantrums he was having per day, as well as the intensity of the tantrum, while I looked at the anecdotal information and asked myself if he was stabilizing or not. Together, we had a pretty clear picture of how Brendan was doing.

If, after you've measured the results of your decision, you find your decision wasn't positive, you do have the right to change course. However, be patient—sometimes it takes a while for decisions to have an impact. When you make your decision—and identify how it will be measured—also schedule a time to check in and decide whether to stay the course or change.

MANAGING SCARCE MONETARY RESOURCES

This topic is too big to cover completely here, but it still needs to be touched upon. Managing money can be a source of stress for any family. This is especially true for the average family raising a child with special needs.

Parenting a child with SPD—or any disorder—can be extremely expensive. Even if you have good health insurance, you'll still be faced with many co-pays for appointments and prescriptions. This can quickly make a large dent in a limited budget. Managing tight finances becomes even more challenging when you choose supports for your child that aren't reimbursed. For example, Brendan has a tutor that he sees every week. This comes to $120 a month. For our budget, that's a lot. Other people we know have chosen private schools for their children. For many families, that's just not possible—or, at least, not possible without a drastic change in lifestyle. How, then, do you address these challenges?

The first step is to understand your feelings about money; these tend to stem from your experiences in your family of origin. I was raised in a family where money wasn't a scarce commodity. We weren't wealthy, but we also didn't have a strict budget. We could do what we wanted without worry about the cost. In high school and college, I didn't have any sense of the value of money—I also didn't have any clue how to make or stick to a budget. To me, money meant freedom. In fact, to me, having a budget equaled a loss of freedom; it was constricting.

In my wife's family, on the other hand, money was very scarce—especially when she was a young child. Money was something that needed to be protected or guarded. It meant security. Even now, it can cause her great pain to spend money.

With the expenses of three children—one with special needs—my wife and I have had to really think about how we perceive money and what's important to us. The following personal reflection can help you think about your own situation. I encourage you and your partner to answer these questions separately, and then discuss them with each other.

Personal Reflection

Did your family of origin have a budget? How was it enforced or followed?

How was money perceived by your parents? What feelings might have been behind this perception?

What does money mean to you now? How do you feel after buying something for yourself, your children, or your partner?

How does your experience in your family of origin impact your perception of money now?

How do your perceptions and feelings about money impact your own family?

Use the communication skills outlined in chapter 3 to discuss the financial issues in your relationship with your partner—especially how your finances are impacted by the special needs of your child. Take it slow—this is an issue that can cause extreme tension and even the breakup of relationships if not handled carefully.

Therapy and intervention don't have to mean high costs and expenses, though they often do. Meaningful supports to therapy can come from participation in simple, homegrown recreational activities.

Local YMCAs and parks-and-recreation departments often have great programs. Karate and Tai Kwan Do are excellent activities for building concentration, gross motor coordination, and balance. Gymnastics is another excellent activity—it, too, builds gross motor coordination, while also providing proprioceptive and vestibular input. After a good gymnastics session, Brendan is calm and relaxed.

My wife, Michelle Auer, the frugal occupational therapist, has put together the following list of inexpensive ways to help support children with SPD outside of traditional therapy. (Although extensive, this isn't a complete list by any means—it's just intended to get you thinking about ways to inexpensively support your child at home.)

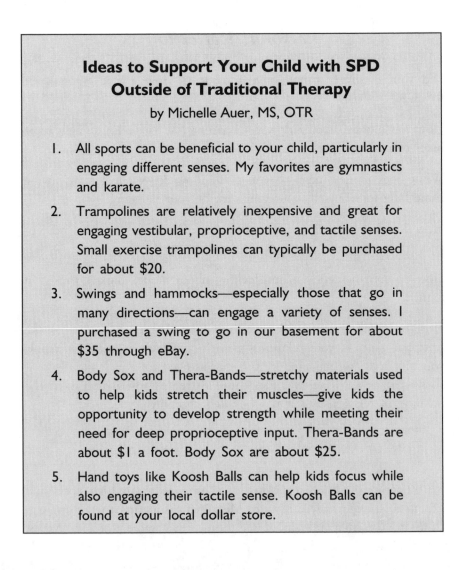

Ideas to Support Your Child with SPD Outside of Traditional Therapy
by Michelle Auer, MS, OTR

1. All sports can be beneficial to your child, particularly in engaging different senses. My favorites are gymnastics and karate.

2. Trampolines are relatively inexpensive and great for engaging vestibular, proprioceptive, and tactile senses. Small exercise trampolines can typically be purchased for about $20.

3. Swings and hammocks—especially those that go in many directions—can engage a variety of senses. I purchased a swing to go in our basement for about $35 through eBay.

4. Body Sox and Thera-Bands—stretchy materials used to help kids stretch their muscles—give kids the opportunity to develop strength while meeting their need for deep proprioceptive input. Thera-Bands are about $1 a foot. Body Sox are about $25.

5. Hand toys like Koosh Balls can help kids focus while also engaging their tactile sense. Koosh Balls can be found at your local dollar store.

6. Big canisters or trays filled with dried beans, rice, or sand can support your child's sensory needs. Add small objects to the bin for your child to find. This activity supports object discrimination and tactile sense. Estimated cost would be around $6 for the canister and beans.

7. Therapy balls are great for kids to roll over, sit on, or bounce on; therapy balls develop strength, balance, and coordination, and engage the vestibular and tactile senses. I found therapy balls on Amazon.com for $10 to 14 each, depending on the size.

8. Aromatherapy can help calm or stimulate a child, depending on the scent. I've found scented candles and oils at the dollar store.

9. Fish tanks (with fish, of course!) can be very calming. I found them at a discount super store starting at about $15 for a small tank, and $1.50 per fish.

10. Rocking horses engage both the vestibular and tactile senses. I found one at a thrift store for about $5.

11. Tents, tubes, and pillow-and-blanket forts can calm the child who is overstimulated by sights and sounds. They can also provide deep, calming proprioception. Pillow-and-blanket forts are free since you probably already have them. Tents and tubes can be purchased at thrift stores for as low as $7 to 10.

12. Chewelry—rubbery plastic bracelets, necklaces, and clip-ons your child can chew—can be purchased through most therapy catalogs for about $5 each.

13. Headphones and earplugs can soothe an oversensitive sense of hearing when necessary. Earplugs are about $2 per pack, while headphones vary greatly in price, depending on the quality and where you get them.

14. Modeling clay, Play-Doh, and putty engage tactile and proprioceptive senses—and sometimes, with scented

dough, even the sense of smell. Brendan's favorite is Flarp putty, purchased at the dollar store, because it adds a sound component. Play dough can also be made at home. An Internet search will provide the recipe.

15. Finger-paint play engages the visual and tactile senses. It can also spark your child's creative talents. Finger paints can be found at your local dollar store or discount retailer from $1 to 4 for up to six small jars.

16. Taking care of a family pet and having your child complete chores at home supports most of the senses—and is free for the most part. (It can't get any better than that!)

While therapy can be extremely expensive, there are many ways to support your child inexpensively. Maybe you can't afford a private school that costs $15,000 a year. That's okay. By doing simple things at home, you can support your child with SPD, while also building a nurturing relationship—something that's far more valuable than any form of therapy. My wife and I have found that it's important to just do what we can; stretching or exceeding our budget to support our children creates stress in our marriage and in us.

FINAL THOUGHTS

In this chapter, we've discussed some ways to cope with the daily stress of parenting a child with SPD, including: getting adequate respite, practicing some form of spirituality or faith, nurturing relationships, living in the moment, and appreciating the little things in life. Tapping into your culture and self-identity can also ground you and provide relief from stress.

We've also talked about the importance of establishing a process for decision making that's unique to your family. Key points to consider in the decision-making process include the influences of your family of origin and culture, and how you will evaluate the outcome of your choices.

In managing monetary resources, we talked again about the influences of your family of origin and how these influences can shape perceptions and feelings about money. Money is a major source of stress for many families; it's especially important for families of children with special needs to keep money issues under control.

Chapter 9

Parting Thoughts

Marine Phosphorescence

The phosphorescent bubbles,
All undisturbed by troubles,
Lie dark, unnoticed in the deep,
'Till breakers toss them starward
Or ship prows push them forward
Or swimmers wake them from their sleep.

So bear the irritation
That makes for radiation
Of light where darkness was before;
And thank the kind Provision
That sends thee rude collision
And makes thy soul to shine the more.

—Frederick S. Miller

There's nothing easy about parenting a child with SPD. Parenting a child with SPD is often frustrating, expensive, and exhausting. The other day, when my wife and I were alone together on a date, we asked each other the terrible question of what life would be like with just Lauren and Evan. We agreed that it would be really easy to parent our two typically-developing children—too easy. As challenging as Brendan is, he also makes everyone in the family laugh, cry, and appreciate our common humanity. Without him, we would be the phosphorescent bubbles of my great-grandfather's poem—but undisturbed by troubles. Brendan adds complexity to our lives, making our souls shine the more.

Susan and I hope that after reading this book, you'll have a deeper appreciation of how sharing your life with a child with SPD can make you a better person and enrich your family. And, too, we hope that you'll accept the importance of your role as parent and become the leader of the team that cares for and supports your special child.

We'll talk about three final, very important issues in this last chapter: the feeling of isolation that often accompanies parenting a child with SPD, the motivation required to truly effect positive changes, and the incredible power of sharing your story.

YOU AREN'T ALONE

It's true that your child with SPD is unique. It's also true that your family's experiences, values, culture, and beliefs are unique. There's no other child in the world like Brendan. There's no other family like yours. But this doesn't mean that you're alone. Remember, approximately 5 percent of children have sensory issues. There are many families like ours—all of whom are looking for support, shared knowledge, guidance, and someone who has "been there, done that." You can find this community by speaking up about your child in your school system, your community, or over the Internet.

What you share with these other families is a bond that crosses all kinds of cultural, economic, and social boundaries. In my role as president of the board of the KID Foundation, I've had the privilege of meeting an incredible number of families with a child with SPD. There's a great diversity among these families: some are incredibly wealthy, while others are short on money but strong in character.

It's amazing, too, who you find just through casual conversation. When I was looking for a Web designer for the Web site connected to this book, my initial contact with a designer was made based solely on her portfolio. When I mentioned the title of the book, she said that she, too, had a child with SPD.

Support Groups

When you contribute to one of the many listservs for parents of children with special needs, or participate in an SPD parent meeting, you get a sense of the common experiences that we all share. It's powerful to know that you're not alone. Your struggles are shared: many parents have difficulty getting enough respite, advocating for their child, providing a nutritious diet, and keeping relationships healthy, all within the constraints of limited financial resources.

There are support groups specifically dedicated to serving Spanish speakers and support groups specifically dedicated to serving people of color. If you're looking for special needs resources dedicated to serving your specific racial, ethnic, or language group, start by asking for information at centers, churches, or other human services agencies in your community. Newspapers specific to your group can also be good sources of information.

The reality is that the overwhelming majority of participants in support groups and listservs are mothers—I am the only male cochair or chair of an SPD Parent Connections group in the world. Fathers may understandably feel isolated. But this doesn't mean that fathers are alone. A variety of resources for fathers is listed in the resources section at the back of this book. Worth highlighting, however, is the Fathers Network (www.fathersnetwork.org). This Web site has both stories written by fathers of children with special needs and resources specifically for fathers of children with special needs.

Also, even though it may initially feel awkward, I urge fathers to participate in listservs and support groups—even when there aren't any other fathers in the group. We need your perspective. And when one father participates, others are more likely to, as well.

One nice thing about listservs and groups is that you can participate as often or as little as you wish. Do whatever meets your needs. By and large, you'll hear from both parents coping with similar challenges and parents who have dealt with these same issues in the past. You'll find a lot of practical tips. Groups can, however, change over time, especially on the Internet. If you're uncomfortable with a particular group, give it a chance. Really get to know its regular members—*then* decide if it's a good fit for you.

People Want to Help

I'm quite open about the challenges and joys of parenting Brendan. As a result, I've found that the vast majority of professionals really do want to help. Because I've spoken openly about his needs, Brendan has received a free, two-hour mental health consultation with a psychiatrist; an expedited comprehensive assessment by a highly regarded university-affiliated program, covered by our insurance (I even got to handpick the specialists); and a free in-home consultation with a behavior specialist. And he has an outstanding tutor because I asked someone I highly respect if she would work with him.

Nonprofit agencies serving children and families as well as churches, schools, counselors, occupational therapists, and hospital social workers also all want to help. Often, in fact, their sole purpose is to help children and families—but they can't help you if you don't let them know what you need. Granted, some individuals and organizations are better at helping than others; don't let one bad experience prevent you from seeking assistance again.

If you express yourself sincerely and with respect, you may be surprised by the assistance that's offered. Remember, too, that rules are sometimes flexible. Specialists may be able to find ways of either going around rules, or bending them a little. Usually, if they want to help, specialists can find the appropriate phrase or code to unlock the necessary doors. Be patient; you may have to ask several times if there's a way to get referred for the specific service you want.

Conferences

Conferences are a great way to meet other parents and professionals with similar interests. At conferences, you can also learn about resources, strategies, and research that may help both your child and your family.

In terms of cost, conferences sponsored by for-profit companies generally won't discount registration fees (although it never hurts to ask). Conferences sponsored by state agencies and parent advocacy programs almost always offer parent scholarships. In my experience, to qualify for these scholarships, you simply have to complete a one-page request. Scholarships are generally available on a first-come, first-served basis, so as soon as you hear about the conference, ask for a scholarship application form from the sponsoring agency. In some cases, the agency may even pay for your lodging—and if you're really lucky, your meals, too.

Your state's developmental disabilities program may also command a pool of funds for parents to attend conferences throughout the state. Usually, you pay for these conferences up front, and get reimbursed from the state afterwards. Again, these funds are usually available on a first-come, first-served basis. Unfortunately, in times of budget constraints these funds are usually the first to go.

Supportive Friends

Friends can help both you and your family feel understood and supported—especially if your friends truly accept your child with SPD and any accompanying challenges. Your children will be able to sense if your friends are truly accepting—if they are, your children will feel secure in the knowledge that your family's uniqueness is okay, that it's not something to hide. They will learn that despite our many surface differences, there are people who not only accept these differences, but also look beyond and value what is in our hearts.

However, the reality is that you may find that some friends—perhaps even those closest to you—aren't accepting of your child with SPD. You may discover this from their limited interactions with your child, questioning looks, or just a sense that they aren't comfortable. Sometimes it can help to explain your child's disorder and provide reassurance that your child is doing the best she can. (You may want to use the elevator speech and other communication tools discussed in chapter 6.)

Eventually, you may discover that a friend just isn't comfortable around children with special needs. If that's the case, you don't have to abandon your friendship. You may, however, have to put some effort into identifying opportunities when you can be with your friend in an environment comfortable to both of you. Your friendship can still continue—it may just need to adapt. You might also have some friends who aren't as close individually, but are great with your family as a whole; they, too, can play an important role in your family's well-being.

Having a child with SPD can also open up a whole new world of possible friendships. You might meet new friends at support groups, therapy appointments, or extracurricular activities for children with special needs. In fact, that's how I met my coauthor, Susan. We first attended professional meetings together, and then discovered that we both had children with SPD. We stayed in contact, and when it came time to write this book, I tapped her on the shoulder. Friendships that start this way can be extraordinary. They can be easier to start, too, because you already know going into them that the other person is going to be accepting of your child's strengths and challenges.

WHY CHANGE?

Unfortunately, reading a book, taking a class, or attending a conference may not help you at all if you don't have a plan to do something with the information you're gathering. In college, I attended a required art history class. Although I found the class interesting for its historical perspective, I didn't find the information I was learning relevant to what I wanted to do with my life. I had absolutely no artistic talent and no interest in developing my knowledge of art. As a result, I can't tell you anything about the history of art. All the information I had to learn in that class was purged from my memory long ago.

Similarly, unless you actively plan to do something with the information you're learning from this book, eventually the information will be purged from your mind. The motivation to use the information you're learning in a meaningful way must come from deep within your heart. Only you can know if you truly are motivated to change.

To make things even more difficult, many of the changes we suggest you make require you to put energy into your family and child with SPD without any guarantee of a payoff—and sometimes without even knowing what's possible. Because you parent your children every day, it can be hard to notice growth. I never realize even how much my children have grown physically until I look at a picture taken in the past.

For me, I find it helps to think of everything that I'm doing today as an investment in what I want for my children. Children grow up very quickly. My daughter Lauren is nine years old—I have only nine years to get her in shape before she goes to college, and twelve with Brendan. I want my kids to have healthy relationships, spirituality, a good education, and the confidence to take on life's many challenges. In my opinion, these are the basics. But I also know that my children may completely surprise me with how far they take themselves.

It also helps to give yourself some credit. By reading this book, you've already demonstrated a certain level of motivation. There was a reason that you chose to pick up this book and read it. Why did you? What were you hoping to accomplish?

Probably, concerns for your child and family were your primary motivating factor. Having read this book, you should now have some tools and strategies you can use to better support your family. The next step is to figure out what actions you will take. Perhaps this book fulfills your immediate needs and now you just want to begin using your new knowledge. If that's the case, you should know that it will take practice and patience. It's good to remember that if you find your family falling back into old habits, you can always come back here and reread sections.

Reading this book may also have brought up some wounds regarding your childhood or marriage. Try to understand these wounds and why they are there. What are their root causes? Don't try to ignore these issues—they won't go away. It's sort of like ignoring a cavity: you can ignore it, but if you do, your tooth will only become more decayed. Once you recognize where the wounds have come from, you may choose to address them yourself. If, however, you find that you're having difficulty addressing issues on your own, it's probably time to call for some external support—contact a mental health professional, member of the clergy, or some other provider that you trust.

What Is Possible?

Throughout this book, I've talked about my experiences with my brother Roger. I've explained that Roger is on the autistic spectrum and how, at an early age, it was recommended that he be placed in the state mental institution. Things truly appeared hopeless when he was five years old or so. He repeated what was said to him in a slow monotone voice; he was aggressive. What I haven't yet mentioned, however, is that Roger, in addition to graduating with a bachelor's degree from Indiana University and living independently, has become one of the top sales associates in his department store. In fact, for the past several years, he has been awarded top recognition honors at work.

You may know that it is extremely unusual for a person with autism to work in a social environment. We believe that Roger has used his extraordinary talent for geography to his advantage; he can tell you exactly where to find any item in his area. During training, he was given a sales script; he follows it exactly, step by step. In many respects, he is a sales manager's dream.

When Roger was five years old, my parents never imagined that he would do so well. So remember: even though your situation may appear dark, you can have no idea of how well your parenting efforts might pay off. The payoff could be extraordinary—well beyond anyone's hopes and dreams.

THE POWER OF SHARING YOUR STORY

Other parents and families want to connect with you. They want to hear your story, and they want to help, because doing so helps them, too. Rhonda (from chapter 8) and I have totally different cultural backgrounds. What we have in common is parenting a child with special needs. We both understand the frustrations and rewards. Because of this commonality, I've been blessed with the opportunity to learn how Rhonda has coped with these challenges—and about her unique cultural perspective. And I think Rhonda has enjoyed sharing her parenting experiences with me, because in doing so it became clear to her how much wisdom she has gained.

My passion for supporting families with children with special needs led to the idea for this book. Two years ago, as I began to write this, all I had was a unique personal perspective of disabilities, the ability to write reasonably well, and a crazy idea to write a book. As I became more involved in writing, my belief in the importance of taking care of the family as a whole grew and grew. Through the process of sharing my story, I've learned about both my shortcomings and my strengths—and more about my family as well.

Susan shares my passion for sharing knowledge. Her own experiences have shown her that many people don't have the information they need to get the best for their child and their family. This book was a great opportunity for her to use her story in a powerful way to help others.

The power that comes from sharing your story is unique to every individual. I can't tell you what return you'll get from sharing your story with others. I can tell you, however, that sharing your story can be emotionally healing for both you and your family.

Sharing your story might also provide just enough inspiration for another couple to work through problems in their relationship, rather than get divorced. Sharing your story might motivate another father to become more involved in the life of his child. Or it might give strength to another mother struggling to keep all of the pieces of life together. Or it might encourage another family to support all of their children, not just the child with SPD.

Ways to Share Your Story

We've already discussed listservs, support groups, and conferences, but how you choose to share your story is really limitless. Don't think that sharing your story has to mean writing or speaking. You can share your story through photography, landscape, sculpture, architecture, quilting, dance, volunteerism, or starting a business or nonprofit. At the right time, you'll find a way to share your story that's meaningful to you. Whatever it is, share it with the world.

If you're into writing, I encourage you to write a book or a blog. The SPD community needs good information. We should have the best books available specifically for SPD. So far, we have a good start, but we need more. We also need people in leadership roles who understand the needs of parents and families. If you're into activism, consider running for school board or some other elected position, or apply for appointment to a state or national commission. If you're feeling a little less ambitious, just talk about SPD with friends, acquaintances, and professionals that you come into contact with. You may discover they're facing similar issues; at the very least, you can help build awareness of SPD.

FINAL THOUGHTS

Although Susan and I have tried to present information gently, a lot of information has been covered. It takes time and commitment to adopt new habits and lifestyle changes. Be patient with yourself. Be patient with your family. Remember: you and your entire family—not just the child with special needs—need recognition and support; everyone in your family has a critical role.

The most important thing to take away from this book may simply be new perspectives. You may now be thinking about your values, your cultural beliefs, and your family in new, different ways. This will help you find a better balance in parenting your children. It can also be quite a shift in thinking to know that all of your children—including your child with special needs—are born with an innate, natural resilience. It's there. You can see it every day.

If Susan and I have achieved our objectives, you now know what to focus on to strengthen your unique family, and how to recognize the gifts that your child with SPD brings. We wish you and your family extraordinary outcomes—outcomes beyond your wildest dreams—and a journey full of memories. As members of the SPD community that we all share, our thoughts are with you.

Resources

We've included in this section information on many Web sites, catalogs, products, books, and other resources that we've either found helpful ourselves or that others have recommended to us. We don't, however, endorse any product or service and this isn't a definitive list of all of the resources on SPD. This listing is intended to be a starting point for your own research; we'd love to hear from you if you find new resources we don't mention here.

We'll start with some general information about two major pieces of legislation that have an impact on children with special needs (the Individuals with Disabilities Education Act and Section 504 of the Rehabilitation Act). We then provide resource information for eleven different topics (arranged alphabetically): fathers, finances, health care, multicultural issues, parent support, related disabilities, relationships, sensory processing disorder, siblings, special education, and stress. We suggest you try several of the resources listed under any topic to find the resource that will work best for you.

OVERVIEW OF THE INDIVIDUALS WITH DISABILITIES EDUCATION ACT

The Individuals with Disabilities Education Act (IDEA), first passed in 1987 and reauthorized in 2004, is designed "to ensure that all children with disabilities have available to them a free appropriate public education that emphasizes special education and related services designed to meet their unique needs and prepare them for further education, employment and independent living . . . and to ensure that the rights of children with disabilities and parents of such children are protected" (Section 1400[d]).

The following points address many of the questions that parents of children with SPD have about IDEA:

- SPD is not a disability covered under IDEA. In general, disability is defined as mental retardation, hearing impairment, speech or language impairment, emotional disturbance, orthopedic impairment, autism, traumatic brain injury, other health impairment, or a specific learning disability. Therefore, in order for your child with SPD to qualify for special education services under IDEA, your child has to display an additional disability that requires such services.

- Parents must provide written consent for an initial IDEA evaluation to occur; this initial evaluation and determination of eligibility must occur within sixty days of receiving parental consent.

- Occupational therapy is considered a related service, not a primary service. This means that there has to be another primary service to which occupational therapy is attached. For example, if your child is diagnosed with a speech/language impairment, speech therapy would then be a primary service. However, your child might also need occupational therapy as a related service to address other aspects of the child's speech/language impairment; this related service might include work on writing, attention, or posture.

- Children covered under IDEA have certain specific legal rights, including due process procedures, protection for behaviors that result from the child's disability, and most importantly the right to a free, appropriate public education with an Individualized Education Plan. The IEP is a legal contract that details the services that the school district is required to provide for the child; parents are required to be active members of the team that develops the IEP.

OVERVIEW OF SECTION 504 OF THE REHABILITATION ACT

Under Section 504 of the Rehabilitation Act, qualifying children are entitled to "the provision of regular or special education and related aids and services that . . . are designed to meet individual educational needs of persons with disabilities as adequately as the needs of persons without disabilities are met." (34 C.F.R. 104.33[b][1]).

A principal or special education teacher is usually designated as a 504 plan coordinator; a written request for a 504 plan should be given to this coordinator. In order to qualify, a child must have a physical or mental impairment that substantially limits at least one major life activity (walking, seeing, hearing, speaking, learning, reading, writing, math, working, caring for oneself, or performing manual tasks).

No services are attached to a 504 plan. Your child cannot receive regular occupational, speech, or other therapy under Section 504. The 504 plan may, however, list accommodations and/or modifications that the school will provide. For example, these might include preferential seating, use of a Thera-Band or special seat cushion, frequent checks for understanding, extended time to complete tests and assignments, and positive reinforcement. These strategies are designed to make it possible for the child to receive an appropriate education, but aren't intended to provide special education or therapy services.

A 504 plan doesn't provide the same procedural protections as the IDEA; a district has many more obligations under IDEA than 504.

For more information about IDEA and 504 plans, we recommend the following Web sites:

www.wrightslaw.com
The overall best reference site on IDEA and legal aspects of special education.

www.ldonline.org/article/6086
An excellent article explaining the differences between IDEA and Section 504.

RESOURCES BY SUBJECT

Fathers

Finances

Health care

Multicultural issues

Parent support

Related disabilities

Relationships

Sensory processing disorder

Siblings

Special education

Stress

Fathers

Web Sites

www.fathersnetwork.org
The Fathers Network has numerous stories from fathers on a broad range of topics, including disabilities. The site's tone is

clearly father-to-father; the site also maintains links to major disabilities resources.

www.nlffi.org/programs.html

The National Latino Fatherhood and Family Institute is one of the few organizations that actually provides a service rather than sells a product. Many worthwhile programs are offered, including a mentoring program; a very good newsletter can be downloaded for free.

www.npnff.org

This is the Web site of the National Practioners Network of Fathers and Families. It is targeted to practitioners who are working to build greater involvement of fathers in their children's lives. The site also maintains a list of fatherhood conferences, as well as a links to all of the major fatherhood organizations.

Books

Lang, G., and J. Lankford-Moran. 2002. *Why a Daughter Needs a Dad: A Hundred Reasons*. Nashville: Cumberland House Press.

Newberger, E. 1999. *The Men They Will Become: The Nature and Nurture of Male Character*. New York: Perseus.

Pruett, K. 2000. *FatherNeed: Why Father Care Is as Essential as Mother Care for Your Child*. New York: Free Press.

Roseman, B. 2001. *A Kid Just Like Me: A Father and Son Overcome the Challenges of ADD and Learning Disabilities*. New York: Perigee.

Stimpson, J. 2004. *Alex: The Fathering of a Preemie*. Chicago: Academy Chicago Publishers.

Finances

Web Sites

www.askmerrill.ml.com

Merrill Lynch has a financial planning program for families with children with special needs, including specially trained advisors.

Click on the financial advisor tab, then view all "advice and planning" products.

www.metlife.com

This Web site of Met Life has a very comprehensive planning section, with sound tips and links to major disability organizations. Click on the individuals tab, then "Life Advice," then "Family," then "About Planning for Your Child or Other Dependent with Special Needs."

www.orientaltrading.com

A good place to shop for items to support your child at home at decent prices; it sells relatively inexpensive crafts, activities, balls, seasonal items, and glow toys.

www.sharedc.org

SHARE is a food program open to everyone. Staffed by volunteers, it uses its collective buying power to purchase food at greatly reduced costs. Typically, by participating in a SHARE program you can save 50 percent on your grocery bill. Click on the links tab for affiliate SHARE programs in your area.

Books

Brock, F. 2005. *Live Well on Less Than You Think: The New York Times Guide to Achieving Your Financial Freedom.* New York: Times Books.

Orman, S. 2000. *9 Steps to Financial Freedom: Practical and Spiritual Steps So You Can Stop Worrying.* New York: Three Rivers Press.

Toohey, B., and M. Toohey. 2001. *The Average Family's Guide to Financial Freedom: How You Can Save a Small Fortune on a Modest Income.* New York: Wiley.

Health Care

Web Sites

www.disabilityinfo.gov

An excellent, easy to use site that compiles information from several different government agencies, forming a one-stop shop for information. A wide variety of topics is covered, including employment, education, housing, transportation, health, benefits, technology, community life, and civil rights.

www.healthinschools.org

The site of the Center for Health and Health Care in Schools, George Washington University Medical Center; a wealth of health information. While much of the information here is pertinent to the parenting of any child, the resources on mental health and psychotropic drugs are particularly valuable for parenting a child with SPD.

www.hispanichealth.org

Web site of the National Alliance for Hispanic Health. Offers a toll-free hotline (1-866-Su-Familia, or 1-866-783-2645), fact sheets, health news, publications, and links. If you have a health- or insurance-related question, this is a great resource.

Multicultural Issues

Web Sites

www.100blackmen.org

100 Black Men of America, Inc., is a philanthropic organization dedicated to serving the African-American community through leadership, mentoring, education, health and wellness, and economic development. Their Wimberly Initiative addresses disproportionality in special education, and a mentoring program serves children with special needs from partnering schools.

www.fiestaeducativa.org

Fiesta Educativa serves Hispanic families with children with special needs. Although based in California, there are also chapters in other states.

www.hispanichealth.org

The National Alliance for Hispanic Health offers a toll-free hotline (1-866-Su-Familia, or 1-866-783-2645), fact sheets, health news, publications, and links. If you have a health- or insurance-related question, this is a great resource.

www.nicwa.org

The National Indian Child Welfare Association runs a variety of initiatives to support families, including a fatherhood project and listservs. Resources also include a tribal directory, library, and information packets.

www.ffcmh.org

The Federation of Families for Children's Mental Health provides great information on culturally proficient, family-centered care. Brochures, books, and other print materials can be downloaded from the site, many for free.

Books

Abboud, S. K., and J. Y. Kim. 2005. *Top of the Class: How Asian Parents Raise High Achievers—and How You Can Too.* New York: Berkley Trade.

Bauermeister, J. 2000. *Hiperactivo, Impulsivo, Distraído—¿Me Conoces?: Guía Acerca del Déficit Atencional para Padres, Maestros y Profesionales.* New York: Guilford Press.

Ladner, J. 2000. *The Ties That Bind: Timeless Values for African American Families.* New York: Wiley.

Vazquez, C. I. 2004. *Parenting with Pride—Latino Style: How to Help Your Child Cherish Your Cultural Values and Succeed in Today's World.* New York: Rayo.

Parent Support

Web Sites

www.beachcenter.org

This site contains an amazing amount of information, from research articles and parent stories to links to all of the Parent to Parent groups across the United States.

www.pacer.org

The Parent Advocacy Coalition for Educational Rights (PACER Center) focuses on parents helping parents; a wide variety of information pertinent to families is provided. This site also maintains an extensive links page, covering a wide range of disabilities and topics.

www.thearc.org

The ARC is a national advocacy organization with chapters in every state; this site offers wonderful information on every topic dealing with children with special needs. Also, parent advocates are available through the ARC to help families work with school systems and legal issues.

Related Disabilities

We can't offer a comprehensive list of resources on all related disabilities here. But here are some good places to look for information on some of the disorders that often involve sensory issues:

Web Sites

www.autism-society.org

The Autism Society of America is the premiere advocacy organization for persons with autism. This site offers both informative content and many useful links.

www.fragilex.org

The National Fragile X Foundation offers a tremendous amount of information. Medical, intervention, and research are just some of the information categories offered. This site also maintains links to parent resource groups across the country.

www.help4adhd.org

The National Resource Center on ADHD; this Web site links to CHADD (Children and Adults with Attention-Deficit/Hyperactivity Disorder) and provides some information in Spanish.

www.ldonline.org

On this site internationally recognized experts in the area of learning disabilities answer questions. The depth and breadth of the information offered is impressive, covering parents, teachers, kids, forums, and resources to name a few.

www.nlda.org
> The Nonverbal Learning Disorders Association maintains an online forum as well as extensive links. A calendar of events is also provided.

www.preemie-l.org
> An international listserv for families of premature babies.

www.prematurity.org
> The sister Web site of above; runs a listserv for parents of preemies who are four or older.

www.zerotothree.org
> The Zero to Three National Center for Infants, Toddlers, and Families offers easily one of the best resources about early childhood. Many, many articles are provided on topics that cover virtually every concern a parent might have.

Books

Davis, D., and M. T. Stein. 2004. *Parenting Your Premature Baby and Child*. Golden, CO: Fulcrum Publishing.

Greenspan, S., S. Wieder, and R. Simons. 1998. *The Child with Special Needs: Encouraging Intellectual and Emotional Growth*. New York: Perseus.

Lavoie, R. 2005. *It's So Much Work to Be Your Friend: Helping the Child with Learning Disabilities Find Social Success*. New York: Touchstone.

Levine, M. 2002. *A Mind at a Time*. New York: Simon & Schuster.

Tracey, A., and D. Maroney. 1999. *Your Premature Baby and Child*. New York: Berkley Books.

Relationships

Web Sites

www.bettermarriages.org
> The Association for Couples in Marriage Enrichment is a national

organization that offers excellent couple retreats, marriage enrich-
ment groups, and conferences.

www.couplecommunication.com

Couple Communication is a popular, research-based marriage
education program.

www.marriagealive.org

Marriage Alive offers fun, exciting weekend workshops and wonderful books.

www.nire.org

Relationship Enhancement is one of the most popular marriage
education programs.

www.prepinc.com

The Prevention and Relationship Enhancement Program (PREP)
is the program created by Susan and her colleagues, Howard
Markman and Scott Stanley. You can order books and videotapes
here, find out about workshops, and read about their research on
marriage.

www.pairs.com

This highly regarded program offers a number of different workshops for couples.

www.smartmarriages.com

This site brings together all of the latest information on marriage
education and support. Included is a directory of programs and an
annual conference that offers training in every marriage program
imaginable! This site also offers a very complete list of books and
articles on all aspects of marriage and relationships.

Books

Markman, H. J., S. M. Stanley, and S. L. Blumberg. 2001. *Fighting for
Your Marriage.* New and Revised. San Francisco: Jossey-Bass.

Markman, H., S. Stanley, S. L. Blumberg, N. Jenkins, and C. Whitely.
2003. *12 Hours to a Great Marriage.* San Francisco: Jossey-Bass.

Whitfield, K., H. Markman, S. Stanley, and S. L. Blumberg. 2001.
Fighting for Your African-American Marriage.) San Francisco:
Jossey-Bass.

Sensory Processing Disorder

Web Sites

www.henryot.com
> This is the site of therapist Diana Henry; she offers telephone consultations at extraordinarily reasonable rates (see site for contact information). However, the primary reason for the inclusion of this site in this resource list is the handbooks she has developed. Of particular interest is her handbook *S. I. Tools for Teens*. Diana is one of the very few therapists focused on the needs of teens with SPD.

www.kidfoundation.org
> The KID Foundation maintains extensive links to the most up-to-date research information found on the Internet, as well as a link to its sister site, www.spdnetwork.org, geared toward parents and therapists. Spdnetwork.org offers contact information for SPD groups around the world, as well as a resource directory.

www.out-of-sync-child.com
> The Web site for the well-known book of the same name by Carol Stock Kranowitz; this site has one of the most extensive resource lists available on the topic of SPD.

www.sensory-processing-disorder.com
> A comprehensive site of resources, tips, and strategies to address SPD; it also includes links to places to purchase equipment, including hammocks and swings. However, this site is focused almost exclusively on children between birth and preschool.

www.sensoryresources.com
> This site maintains a catalog of products specifically for families with children with SPD. Sensory Resources also sponsors many conferences featuring well-known authorities in SPD.

www.sensorysmarts.com
> The Web site of the authors of *Raising a Sensory Smart Child* (2005); it offers tips to help your child with a variety of behaviors and needs—including excellent suggestions for a sensory diet—as well as recommended books and links.

www.spdresources.com
> This is Chris's Web site; it offers information on finding inexpensive resources for your home, a free newsletter, and information about occupational therapy—including hippotherapy as a service for children with SPD.

Books

Biel, L., and N. Peske. 2005. *Raising a Sensory Smart Child: The Definitive Handbook for Helping Your Child with Sensory Integration Issues.* New York: Penguin.

Kranowitz, C. 2005. *The Out-of-Sync Child: Recognizing and Coping with Sensory Processing Disorder.* Rev. ed. New York: Perigee.

Kranowitz, C., and T. J. Wylie. 2003. *The Out-of-Sync Child Has Fun: Activities for Kids with Sensory Integration Dysfunction.* New York: Perigee.

Miller, L. J., and D. Fuller. 2006. *Sensational Kids: Hope and Help for Children with Sensory Processing Disorder.* New York: Putnam.

Magazines

S. I. Focus
> A magazine dedicated to promoting awareness and understanding of SPD. Ideas, research, and information are presented in understandable terms. Appropriate for parents, but also of interest to therapists. Magazine and subscription information can be found at www.sifocus.com.

Siblings

Web Sites

www.familyvillage.wisc.edu
> Although this Web site focuses primarily on global information about disabilities, information on sibling resources can be found under the family resources tab; this is also an excellent site for information on estate planning and other important topics.

www.thearc.org/siblingsupport

> Perhaps the only Web site solely dedicated to serving brothers and sisters. The site also maintains two listservs: SibKids and SibNet. SibKids is focused on children, SibNet on adult siblings.

Books

Faber, A., and E. Mazlish. 1998. *Siblings Without Rivalry: How to Help Your Children Live Together So You Can Live Too.* New York: Collins.

Faber, A., and E. Mazlish. 1999. *How to Talk So Kids Will Listen and Listen So Kids Will Talk.* New York: Collins.

Meyer, D., and D. Gallagher. 2005. *The Sibling Slam Book: What It's Really Like to Have a Brother or Sister with Special Needs.* Bethesda, MD: Woodbine House.

Meyer, D., and C. Pillo. 1997. *Views from Our Shoes: Growing Up with a Brother or Sister with Special Needs.* Bethesda, MD: Woodbine House.

Special Education

Web Sites

www.ed.gov/policy/speced/guid/idea/idea2004.html

> The U.S. Department of Education's Special Education and Rehabilitative Services Web site for IDEA 2004 resources. You'll find news and information on the Individuals with Disabilities Education Act of 2004 (IDEA), the federal act mandated to improve educational facilities for infants, toddlers, children, and youth with disabilities.

www.wrightslaw.com

> An excellent resource for understanding special education laws and regulations.

www.cec.sped.org

> The Council for Exceptional Children (CEC) is the largest international professional organization dedicated to improving educational outcomes for individuals with exceptionalities: students

with disabilities and the gifted. CEC advocates for appropriate governmental policies, sets professional standards, provides continual professional development, advocates for underserved individuals with exceptionalities, and helps professionals obtain conditions and resources necessary for effective professional practice.

We also recommend you visit the Web site of your state department of education for information on special education services in your state.

Books

Wilmhurst, L., and A. Brue. 2005. *A Parent's Guide to Special Education: Insider Advice on How to Navigate the System and Help Your Child Succeed.* New York: Amacom.

Winter, J. 2006. *Breakthrough Parenting for Children with Special Needs: Raising the Bar of Expectations.* San Francisco: Jossey-Bass.

Wright, P., and P. Wright. 2006. *Wrightslaw: From Emotions to Advocacy: The Special Education Survival Guide.* 2nd ed. Hartfield, VA: Harbor House Law Press.

Magazines

Exceptional Parent Magazine
Offers information on a wide variety of topics, all pertinent to the parent of a child with special needs. Magazine and subscription information can be found at www.eparent.com.

Stress

Web Sites

www.archrespite.org
The ARCH National Respite Network is a very comprehensive resource covering all aspects of respite; fact sheets are available at this site. The site also includes the National Respite Locator Service to search for local programs.

www.childdevelopmentinfo.com/parenting/stress.shtml
Concise, practical tips for reducing parental stress.

www.holistic-online.com/stress
A Web site with an alternative medicine slant; this site offers a lot of information and practical tips for managing stress.

www.specialneedsfamilyfun.com
Despite the presence of annoying ads, this Web site has a lot of information to offer; it focuses on reducing the stress of the entire family.

Books

Carlson, R. 2001. *The Don't Sweat Guide for Parents: Reduce Stress and Enjoy Your Kids More.* New York: Don't Sweat Press.

Davis, M., M. McKay, and E. R. Eshelman. 2000. *The Relaxation and Stress Reduction Workbook.* Oakland, CA: New Harbinger Publications.

References

Ahn, R. R., L. J. Miller, S. Milberger, and D. N. McIntosh. 2004. Prevalence of parents' perceptions of sensory processing disorders among kindergarten children. *American Journal of Occupational Therapy* 58(3):287-293.

Bertone, A., L. Mottron, P. Jelenic, and J. Faubert. 2003. Motion perception in autism: A complex issue. *Journal of Cognitive Neuroscience* 15:218-225.

Center for Research on Child Wellbeing and Social Indicators Survey Center. 2004. Unmarried African-American fathers' involvement with their infants: The role of couple relationships. *Fragile Families Research Brief* 21:1-3.

Covey, S. 1989. *The Seven Habits of Highly Effective People*. New York: Simon & Schuster.

Erickson, M. F., and E. G. Aird. 2005. *The Motherhood Study: Fresh Insights on Mothers' Attitudes and Concerns*. Institute for American Values. (Paper available at www.motherhoodproject.org.)

Feral, C.-H. 1999. Connectedness and development—a theory. Is ecopsychology the answer to emotional well-being? Paper presented at the March meeting of the National Association of School Psychologists, New Orleans, LA. (Paper available at eric.ed.gov, ERIC# ED438489.)

Garmezy, N., and A. S. Masten. 1991. The protective role of competence indicators in children at risk. In *Life-Span Developmental Psychology: Perspectives on Stress and Coping*, edited by E. M. Cummings, A. L. Greene, and K. H. Karraker. Hillsdale, NJ: Lawrence Erlbaum Publishers.

Goldman, L. S., M. Genel, R. J. Bezman, and P. J. Slanetz. 1998. Diagnosis and treatment of attention-deficit/hyperactivity disorder in children and adolescents. Council on Scientific Affairs, American Medical Association. *Journal of the American Medical Association* 279(14):1100-1107.

Hack, M., D. Flannery, M. Schlucter, L. Cartar, E. Borawski, and N. Klein. 2002. Outcomes in young adulthood for very low birth weight infants. *New England Journal of Medicine* 346(3):149-157.

Hanft, B. E., L. J. Miller, and S. J. Lane. 2000. Toward a consensus in terminology in sensory integration theory and practice: Part 3: Observable behaviors: Sensory integration dysfunction. *Sensory Integration Special Interest Section Quarterly* 23(3):1-4.

Havens, C. A. 2005. Becoming a resilient family: Child disability and the family system. *Access Today*, Special Volume, Issue 17.

Kinnealey, M., and L. J. Miller. 1993. Sensory integration/learning disabilities. In *Willard and Spackman's Occupational Therapy*, 8th ed., edited by H. L. Hopkins and H. D. Smith. Philadelphia: J. B. Lippincott Co.

Kupper, L. 1993. Parenting a child with special needs: A guide to readings and resources. *NICHY News Digest* 3(1):1-25.

Lavoie, R. 1994. Do's and don't's for fostering social competence. Originally published in *Learning Disabilities and Social Skills*. Retrieved from www.ldonline.com on February 22, 2006.

Louv, R. 2005. *Last Child in the Woods: Saving Our Children from Nature-Deficit Disorder*. Chapel Hill, NC: Algonquin Books.

Miller, L. J., D. N. McIntosh, J. McGrath, V. Shyu, M. Laupe, A. K. Taylor, F. Tassone, K. Neitzel, T. Stackhouse, and R. J. Hagerman. 1999. Electrodermal responses to sensory stimuli in individuals with fragile X syndrome: A preliminary report. *American Journal of Medical Genetics* 83(4):268-279.

Miller, L. J., J. Reisman, D. N. McIntosh, and J. Simon. 2001. An ecological model of sensory modulation: Performance of children with fragile X syndrome, autism, attention-deficit/hyperactivity disorder, and sensory modulation dysfunction. In *Understanding the Nature of Sensory Integration with Diverse Populations*, edited by S. S. Roley, E. I. Blanche, and R. C. Schaaf. San Antonio, TX: Therapy Skill Builders.

Parush, S., H. Sohmer, A. Steinberg, and M. Kaitz. 1997. Somatosensory functioning in children with attention-deficit/hyperactivity disorder. *Developmental Medicine and Child Neurology* 39: 464-468.

Roehlkepartain, E. C., P. Scales, J. Roehlkepartain, and S. Rude. *Building Strong Families: An In-Depth Report on a Preliminary Survey on What Parents Need to Succeed.* YMCA of the USA and Search Institute. (Paper available at www.searchinstitute.org.)

Rosenthal-Malek, A., and S. Mitchell. 1997. Brief report: The effects of exercise on the self-stimulatory behaviors and positive responding of adolescents with autism. *Journal of Autism and Developmental Disorders* 27(2):193-202.

Schilling, D. L. D., and I. S. D. Schwartz. 2003. Classroom seating for children with attention-deficit/hyperactivity disorder: Therapy balls versus chairs. *American Journal of Occupational Therapy* 57: 534-541.

Summers, J. A., S. K. Behr, and A. P. Turnbull. 1988. Positive adaptation and coping strengths of families who have children with disabilities. In *Support for Caregiving Families: Enabling Positive Adaptation to Disability*, edited by G. H. S. Singer and L. K. Irvin. Baltimore, MD: Brookes.

TeKolste, K., J. Bragg, and S. Wendel, eds. 2004. Extremely Low Birth Weight NICU Graduate Supplement to the *Critical Elements of*

Care for the Low Birth Weight Neonatal Intensive Care Graduate. (Paper available at www.medicalhome.org.)

Wang, J., Y. Wang, and Y. Ren. 2003. A case controlled study on balance function of attention-deficit/hyperactivity disorder (ADHD) children. *Beijing Da Xue Xue Bao* 35:280-283.

Wolin, S., and S. Wolin. 1997. Shifting paradigms: Easier said than done. *Resiliency in Action* (Fall).

Christopher R. Auer, MA, is employed in the Mayor's Office for Education and Children as the disabilities and mental health administrator for Denver's Great Kids Head Start. He is a board member of the Foundation for Knowledge in Development (KID Foundation), founded by Lucy Jane Miller, and was appointed by the governor of Colorado to the Colorado Interagency Coordinating Council, which oversees disability services to children birth to three throughout the state. He holds licensure as a director of special education and is the parent of three children, one of whom is diagnosed with attention-deficit/hyperactivity disorder and sensory processing disorder.

Susan L. Blumberg, Ph.D., is coauthor of six books, including *Fighting for Your Marriage* and *Twelve Hours to a Great Marriage.* She has more than twenty years' experience as a family advocate for families with children with special needs, helping families navigate through the system to obtain services and supports. She has been a member of the board of directors for Denver Early Childhood Connections, the Part C agency for Denver, since 1997 and served as president or vice president for five years. Blumberg received her doctorate in child clinical psychology from the University of Denver in 1991 and is a licensed clinical psychologist. She is also the parent of two children, one of whom is diagnosed with nonverbal learning disability and sensory processing disorder.

Foreword writer **Lucy Jane Miller, Ph.D., OTR,** is associate clinical professor at the University of Colorado Medical School and founder and director of KID Foundation—the only full-time SPD research program in the world—and the Sensory Therapies and Research (STAR) Center for children and adults. She is author of *Sensational Kids: Hope and Help for Children with Sensory Processing Disorder.*

more titles for children with special needs
from new**harbinger**publications

 **The Gift of ADHD**

$14.95 • Item Code: 3899

 **Helping Your Child Overcome an Eating Disorder**

$16.95 • Item Code: 3104

 **Helping Your Depressed Child**

$14.95 • Item Code: 3228

 **Helping Your Child with Selective Mutism**

$14.95 • Item Code: 416X

Helping a Child with Nonverbal Learning Disorder or Asperger's Syndrome

$14.95 • Item Code: 2779

 **Helping Your Child Overcome Separation Anxiety or School Refusal**

$14.95 • Item Code: 4313

 **Helping Your Anxious Child**

$14.95 • Item Code: 1918

 **When Your Child Is Cutting**

$15.95 • Item Code: 4372

 **Helping Your Child with Autism Spectrum Disorder**

$17.95 • Item Code: 3848

 **Helping Your Child with OCD**

$19.95 • Item Code: 3325

 available from new**harbinger**publications
and fine booksellers everywhere

To order, call toll free **1-800-748-6273** or visit our online bookstore at **www.newharbinger.com**

(V, MC, AMEX • prices subject to change without notice)